SUPREME COURT WATCH 2005

Highlights of the 2004 Term
Preview of the 2005 Term

DAVID M. O'BRIEN
UNIVERSITY OF VIRGINIA

W • W • NORTON & COMPANY • NEW YORK • LONDON

W. W. Norton & Company has been independent since its founding in 1923, when William Warder Norton and Mary D. Herter Norton first published lectures delivered at the People's Institute, the adult education division of New York City's Cooper Union. The Nortons soon expanded their program beyond the Institute, publishing books by celebrated academics from America and abroad. By mid-century, the two major pillars of Norton's publishing program—trade books and college texts—were firmly established. In the 1950s, the Norton family transferred control of the company to its employees, and today—with a staff of four hundred and a comparable number of trade, college, and professional titles published each year—W. W. Norton & Company stands as the largest and oldest publishing house owned wholly by its employees.

Printed in the United States of America.

Composition by Cathy Lombardi.
Manufacturing by Victor Graphics, Inc.
Production manager: Benjamin Reynolds.

ISBN 0-393-92818-7 (pbk.)

W. W. Norton & Company, Inc., 500 Fifth Avenue, New York, NY 10110
wwnorton.com

W. W. Norton & Company Ltd., Castle House, 75/76 Wells Street, London W1T 3QT

1 2 3 4 5 6 7 8 9 0

Contents

Preface

Supreme Court Watch 2005 examines the changes and decisions made during the Supreme Court's 2004–2005 term. In addition to highlighting the major constitutional rulings in excerpts from leading cases, I discuss in section-by-section introductions other important decisions and analyze recent developments in various areas of constitutional law. I also preview here the important cases that the Court has granted review and will decide in its 2005–2006 term. To offer even more information in an efficient format, special boxes titled "The Development of Law," "In Comparative Perspective," and "Inside the Court" are also included.

The favorable reception of previous editions of the *Watch* has been gratifying, and I hope that this fifteenth edition will further contribute to students' understanding of constitutional law, politics, and history, as well as to their appreciation for how the politics of constitutional interpretation turns on differing interpretations of constitutional politics and the role of the Supreme Court. I am most grateful to Aaron Javsicas for doing a terrific and expeditious job in producing this edition.

D.M.O.
June 29, 2005

Supreme Court Watch 2005

VOLUME ONE

2

Law and Politics in the Supreme Court: Jurisdiction and Decision-Making Process

Continuing a decade-old trend, in its 2004–2005 term the Rehnquist Court granted and decided by written opinion less than 1 percent of its total docket, giving plenary consideration to 72 cases and summarily deciding with full opinions another five cases (see the "Inside the Court" boxes in this chapter). As usual, the Court more often reversed than affirmed the following decisions.

The Court's Disposition of Appeals in the 2004 Term

	Affirmed	Reversed or Vacated
First Circuit		3
Second Circuit		
Third Circuist	1	2
Fourth Circuit	1	3
Fifth Circuit	2	5
Sixth Circuit	3	7
Seventh Circuit	2	
Eighth Circuit	1	3
Ninth Circuit	2	17
Tenth Circuit		3
Eleventh Circuit	4	4
Federal Circuit		1
District of Columbia Circuit		
Other Federal Courts		
State Courts and Other	4	8
*Totals:	20	56

*Excludes cases decided on original jurisdiction or dismissed for lack of jurisdiction and remanded.

Throughout the 2004–2005 term, speculation mounted that Chief Justice William H. Rehnquist would retire. About to turn 81 years old, he had served on the Court for 33 years and as chief justice for 19 years. Undergoing treatment for thyroid cancer, he missed several months of the Court's oral argument sessions but participated in cases in which the other justices split four to four. But four days after the end of the term, Justice Sandra Day O'Connor sent President George W. Bush a letter informing him of her retirement upon the nomination and the Senate's confirmation of her successor. Appointed in 1981 by Republican President Ronald Reagan, who in his 1980 presidential campaign promised to name the first woman to the Court, Justice

O'Connor served 24 years and in the last decade became the pivotal, "swing," vote on some of the most hotly contested social-civil rights issues. In the last decade, Justice O'Connor was in the majority in 148 out of 193 cases decided by a bare majority, and wrote the opinion for the Court in 25 of those decisions.

Justice O'Connor generally voted with other conservatives to limit congressional power, in defense of federalism. She delivered the Court's opinion in *New York v. United States*, 505 U.S. 144 (1992) (excerpted in Vol. 1, Ch. 7), and joined the majority in other leading rulings, including *United States v. Lopez*, 514 U.S. 549 (1995) (excerpted in Vol. 1, Ch. 6); *Printz v. United States*, 521 U.S. 898 (1997) (excerpted in Vol. 1, Ch. 7); and *United States v. Morrison*, 529 U.S. 598 (2000) (excerpted in Vol. 1, Ch. 6). Justice O'Connor also joined bare majorities in enforcing the Eleventh Amendment to limit congressional power in *Seminole Tribe of Florida v. Florida*, 517 U.S. 44 (1996) (excerpted in Vol. 1, Ch. 7), and *Alden v. Maine*, 527 U.S. 706 (1999) (excerpted in Vol. 1, Ch. 7), among other decisions. But she eventually voted to uphold Congress's power to abrogate states' sovereign immunity from private lawsuits brought under the Family and Medical Leave Act, in *Nevada Department of Human Resources v. Hibbs*, 538 U.S. 721 (2003) (excerpted in Vol. 1, Ch. 7); and under the Americans with Disabilities Act, in *Tennessee v. Lane*, 124 S.Ct. 1978 (2004). Justice O'Connor also generally voted with conservatives in cases involving the rights of the accused and the death penalty, though she issued a bitter dissent from the bare majority's upholding of random drug tests for students in *Board of Education of Independent School District No. 92 of Pottawatomie City v. Earls*, 536 U.S. 822 (2002) (excerpted in Vol. 2, Ch. 7). Likewise, although generally voting with the conservative block to strike down most affirmative-action programs, Justice O'Connor ruled that race may be taken into consideration in order to achieve diverse student bodies in colleges and universities, in *Grutter v. Bollinger*, 539 U.S. 306 (2003) (excerpted in Vol. 2, Ch. 12); as well as in congressional redistricting, in *Hunt v. Cromartie*, 532 U.S. 234 (2001) (excerpted in Vol. 1, Ch. 8).

During her tenure, Justice O'Connor sided with liberal and left-of-center justices to affirm *Roe v. Wade*, 410 U.S. 113 (1973) (excerpted in Vol. 2, Ch. 11), in *Planned Parenthood of Southeastern Pennsylvania v. Casey*, 505 U.S. 833 (1992) (excerpted in Vol. 2, Ch. 11), and to strike down bans on "partial-birth abortions," in *Stenberg v. Carhart*, 530 U.S. 914 (2000) (excerpted in Vol. 2, Ch. 11), as well as joined the majority to strike down laws criminalizing homosexual sodomy in *Lawrence v. Texas*, 539 U.S. 558 (2003) (excerpted in Vol. 2, Ch. 11). Last term, Justice O'Connor voted to hold the First Amendment to bar state and local governments from posting the Ten Commandments in courthouses in *McCreary v. American Civil Liberties Union of Kentucky* (2005) (excerpted below in Vol. 2, Ch 5). Hence, despite her generally conservative record, including siding with the bare majority in *Bush v. Gore*, 531 U.S. 98 (2000), which ended the Florida election recount and effectively decided the presidential election, because of those and other votes Justice O'Connor remained a disappointment for "movement conservatives."

The last time a pivotal justice retired and the balance of the Court shifted was in 1987, when Justice Lewis F. Powell, Jr., stepped down. At the time, he also cast the crucial votes on abortion, affirmative action, and some other controversial issues. President Reagan's nomination to fill his seat of a hard-line conservative, Judge Robert H. Bork, sparked a bitter confirmation battle that resulted in defeat and led to the appointment of a more moderate conservative, Justice Anthony Kennedy.

A little over two weeks after Justice O'Connor announced her retirement, President Bush nominated Court of Appeals for the District of Columbia Circuit Judge John G. Roberts to fill her seat. In that time, conservatives mounted opposition to the possible nomination of the president's friend, Attorney General Alberto Gonzales, as the first Hispanic to sit on the Court. Liberal groups in turn raised funds to wage a media campaign against any hard-line conservative nominee. Bush told both sides to tone down their rhetoric. Speculation grew that Chief Justice Rehnquist might still retire and give Bush strategic opportunities to fill more vacancies, until the chief finally announced that he would stay as long as his health permitted. There was also increasing speculation that Justice O'Connor's seat might be filled by elevating one of two conservative Court of Appeals for the Fifth Circuit judges—

either Judge Edith Brown Clement, whom Bush put on the bench in 2001 but was viewed as not reliably conservative enough; or Judge Edith Jones, who was considered but passed over in 1991 because of controversy over her outspoken opposition to *Roe v. Wade*. Bush narrowed a list of eleven finalists and interviewed five; besides Judge Roberts, Bush met with Judges Clement and Jones, along with Court of Appeals for the Fourth Circuit Judges Michael Luttig and J. Harvie Wilkinson. When announcing his choice, Bush declared that Judge Roberts would interpret the Constitution "strictly" and "not legislate from the bench."

In naming Judge Roberts, Bush satisfied his conservative base, which predicted that the Court's balance would shift to the right. On the other hand, the selection of Judge Roberts over others with longer, more hard-line judicial records, such as Judge Luttig, made it more difficult for Democratic senators initially to voice staunch opposition. A graduate of Harvard College and Harvard Law School, Judge Roberts served on the appellate bench for just two years and had written few opinions. Following law school, he served as a law clerk to then-Associate Justice Rehnquist, before moving into the administration of President Ronald Reagan, first as special assistant to the attorney general and later as associate counsel to the president. After a few years in private practice, he became a deputy solicitor general in the administration of President George H. W. Bush, who nominated him in 1992 to the federal bench but a Senate confirmation vote was never taken. Subsequently, following another eight years in private practice, Roberts was nominated by President George W. Bush to the appellate bench in 2001; after the nomination was blocked by Senate Democrats, Bush renominated Roberts in 2003; he was then confirmed by the Senate without a roll call vote. Throughout his career (eleven years in government service and thirteen in private practice), Judge Roberts earned a reputation within Washington legal circles as a solid conservative and a skillful Supreme Court litigator, arguing 39 cases before the Court and winning 25 of them. In anticipation of the Senate Judiciary's confirmation hearing in September 2005, interest groups for and against him mobilized supporters through emails, Web sites, and direct mail and television ads.

A | *Jurisdiction and Justiciable Controversies*

■ THE DEVELOPMENT OF LAW

Class Action Suits

In February 2005, President George W. Bush signed into law the Class Action Fairness Act, which moves from state courts to federal courts large, interstate class action lawsuits brought by consumers against businesses for fraud or faulty products. For over a decade business groups had lobbied for the legislation. They contended that business faced too many frivolous lawsuits, excessive punitive damage awards, and that lawyers filed such suits in states known to be more favorable to consumers. Consumer advocates, trial lawyers, and the U.S. Judicial Conference opposed the law. They countered that the law would burden the federal judiciary; that federal courts are ill equipped to deal with such suits, which usually involve the application of state consumer-protection laws; and that consumers would be discouraged from bringing such suits.

Under the law, class action suits seeking $5 million or more would remain in state courts only if the primary defendant and more than one-third of the plaintiffs are from the same state. If fewer than one-third of the plaintiffs are from the same state as the primary defendant, and more than $5 million is sought, the case would go to a federal court. In addition, the law also limits attorney fees when plaintiffs only receive discount coupons on products, instead of financial settlements, by linking the fees to the coupon's redemption rate or the actual hours spent working on the case.

B | *The Court's Docket and Screening Cases*

■ Inside the Court

The Business of the Supreme Court in the 2004–2005 Term

SUBJECT OF COURT OPINIONS*	SUMMARY	PLENARY
Admiralty		2
Antitrust		
Bankruptcy		1
Bill of Rights (other than rights of accused) and Equal Protection	1	8
Commerce Clause		
1. Constitutionality and construction of federal regulation		3
2. Constitutionality of state regulation		2
Common Law		1
Miscellaneous Statutory Construction		14
Due process		
1. Economic interests		1
2. Procedure and rights of accused	2	18
3. Substantive due process (noneconomic)	1	
Impairment of Contract and Just Compensation		
International Law, War, and Peace		
Jurisdiction, Procedure, and Practice		13
Land Legislation	1	1
Native Americans		2
Patents, Copyright, and Trademarks		3
Other Suits against the Government		2
Suits by States		
Taxation (federal and state)		1
Totals	5	72

*Note: The classification of cases is that of the author and necessarily invites differences of opinion as to the dominant issue in some cases. The table includes opinions in cases whether decided summarily or given plenary consideration, but not cases summarily disposed of by simple orders, opinions dissenting from the denial of review, and those dismissing cases as improvidently granted.

H | *Opinion Days and Communicating Decisions*

■ INSIDE THE COURT

*Opinion Writing during the 2004–2005 Term**

OPINIONS	MAJORITY	CONCURRING	DISSENTING	SEPARATE	TOTALS
Per Curiam	4				4
Rehnquist	6	1	1	1	9
Stevens	8	7	12		27
O'Connor	8	5	5		18
Scalia	9	8	6	2	25
Kennedy	9	4	4		17
Souter	8	4	6		18
Thomas	8	9	12	3	32
Ginsburg	8	4	7		19
Breyer	10	11	3	1	25
Totals	78	53	56	7	194

*Court opinions disposing of two or more companion cases are counted only once here. In addition, this table includes opinions in cases disposed of either summarily or upon plenary consideration, but does not include cases summarily disposed of by simple orders or concurring or dissenting opinions from the denial of *certiorari*. Two opinions for the Court were delivered in *United States v. Booker* by Justices Stevens and Breyer, and are each counted here as majority opinions.

3

Presidential Power, the Rule of Law, and Foreign Affairs

D | *War-Making and Emergency Powers*

In its 2005-2006 term, the Court will rule on the constitutionality of the "Solomon Amendment," a federal law requiring the cutoff of federal funds to colleges that refuse to permit military recruiters equal access to their students. The Bush administration appealed the case to the Court, arguing that its power to wage war is impaired by colleges and law schools' refusal to admit recruiters from the armed services. Many law schools ban military recruiters because of the government's ban on openly homosexuals in the military services. They have long done so based on a policy of nondiscrimination on the basis of sexual orientation and have also barred corporate and other recruiters for employers who discriminate against homosexuals. The Court of Appeals for the Third Circuit barred the enforcement of the Solomon Amendment, finding it likely that the challengers would win their First Amendment challenge to the law, but stayed its ruling pending the government's appeal. The government's petition asks: "Whether the court of appeals erred in holding that the Solomon Amendment's equal access condition on federal funding likely violates the First Amendment to the Constitution and in directing a preliminary injunction to be issued against its enforcement?" The case is *Rumsfeld v. Forum for Academic and Institutional Rights* (No. 04-1152). In a separate suit against Yale Law School, a federal district court struck down the

Solomon Amendment. In that case, *Burt v. Rumsfeld* (No. 04-1434), law school faculty filed a petition to the Court, asking it to grant the case before the Court of Appeals for the Second Circuit reviews it.

■ IN COMPARATIVE PERSPECTIVE

The House of Lords Rules Against the Indefinite Detention of Terrorists

As a result of the continued conflicts in North Ireland, the United Kingdom enacted the Terrorism Act of 2000, which broadened the definition of terrorism, prohibited fundraising for terrorist organizations, and expanded law enforcement powers to stop, search, arrest, and detain suspected terrorists. But, after the international terrorist attacks on September 11, 2001, on the Twin Towers and the Pentagon, the Parliament enacted the Anti-Terrorism, Crime, and Security Act of 2001, which, among other things, derogated obligations under Article 5 of the European Convention on Human Rights that prohibit detention without trial.

The provisions of the Anti-Terrorism, Crime, and Security Act were subsequently challenged and the House of Lords, in an eight-to-one decision, in *A(FC) and others (FC) v. Secretary of State for the Home Department,* [2004] UKHL 56, held that indefinite detention of suspected terrorists without charge or trial violates Articles 5 and 14 of the European Convention on Human Rights, issuing a "declaration of incompatibility" (since English courts have no power to invalidate legislation), and referring the matter back to Parliament. Lord Bingham issued the lead opinion and found that the flaw in the detention policy was the way it discriminated against foreign nations. In his words:

> The appellants share certain common characteristics which are central to their appeals. All are foreign (non-UK) nationals. None has been subject of any criminal charge. In none of their cases is a criminal trial in prospect. All challenge the lawfulness of their detention. More specifically, they all contend that such detention was inconsistent with obligations binding on the United Kingdom under the European Convention on Human Rights. . . .
>
> The appellants were treated differently from both suspected international terrorists who were not UK nationals but could be removed and also from suspected international terrorists who were UK nationals and could not be removed. There can be no doubt but that the difference in treatment was on grounds of nationality or immigration status (one of the proscribed grounds under Article 14).

Lord Walker, the lone dissenter, countered that:

> The appropriate intensity of scrutiny of decisions in this crucial area—involving both national security and individual rights—presents a dilemma. . . . The court should show a high degree of respect for the Secretary of State's appreciation, based on secret intelligence sources, of the security risks; but at the same time the court should subject to a very close scrutiny the practical effect which derogating measures have on human rights, the importance of the rights affected, and the robustness of any safeguards intended to minimize the impact of the derogating measures on individual human rights.

In 2005, Parliament enacted a new anti-terrorism act that authorizes judges to impose a range of restrictions on terrorist suspects, short of imprisonment, including placing them under house arrest, imposing nighttime curfews, requiring electronic tagging, and barring their use of cell phones and computers. The law will expire in 2006.

6

Congress: Legislative, Taxing, and Spending Powers

C | *From the New Deal Crisis to the Administrative State*

In *Gonzales v. Raich* (excerpted below), the Court upheld congressional power and the federal prosecution of users of medicinal marijuana over a challenge that Congress exceeded its powers and the boundaries of federalism. Ten states have legalized the medicinal use of marijuana, but writing for the Court Justice Stevens upheld congressional power to criminalize such use. Chief Justice Rehnquist and Justices O'Connor and Thomas dissented.

In a related controversy, during its 2005–2006 term the Court will consider whether federal law and regulations override state laws permitting physician-assisted suicide, in *Gonzales v. Oregon* (No. 04-0623). In 1994, Oregon voters approved the Death with Dignity Act, enabling physicians to legally prescribe certain lethal substances to assist in the painless death of competent but terminally-ill individuals. In 2001, however, Attorney General John Ashcroft issued a directive under which doctors who proscribe controlled substances to assist suicides may have revoked their registration to distribute such substances, under the Controlled Substances Act of 1970, and criminally prosecuted for violating federal law. He claimed that doctor-assisted suicide was not a "legitimate medical purpose" justifying the prescription of a controlled substance, and that doctor-assisted suicide was "inconsistent with the public interest." A doctor, a group of terminally-ill individuals, and the state of Oregon successfully challenged Ashcroft's directive in a federal district court and that decision was affirmed by the Court of Appeals for the Ninth Circuit. The Department of Justice appealed that decision, arguing that the CSA and general principles of federalism requires a single-national standard, and that doctor-assisted suicide is "fundamentally incompatible with the physician's role as a healer." In response, Oregon asserts "states' rights" and its power to regulate medicine, in maintaining that the federal government exceeded its power.

Gonzales v. Raich

125 S.Ct. 2195 (2005)

Two seriously ill Californians, Angel McClary Raich and Diane Monson, use marijuana for medicinal purposes. Under California's Compassionate Use Act of 1996, they could legally do so; nine other states have similar laws. Raich received her marijuana free of charge from her caregivers, while Monson cultivated her own in the backyard. In 2002, deputies from the Butte County sheriff's department and federal Drug Enforcement Agency (DEA) agents arrived at Monson's home. The sheriff's deputies determined that Monson's cultivation and use of marijuana was legal under state law. But the DEA agents and the U.S. Attorney for the Eastern District of California contended that Monson was in violation of the federal Controlled Substances Act (CSA), which designates marijuana as a Schedule I "controlled substance" and makes it unlawful to possess, manufacture, or distribute such substances. After a three-hour standoff between the Butte County district attorney and the U.S. attorney, the DEA agents seized and destroyed Monson's cannabis plants. Subsequently, Raich and Monson filed a lawsuit and sought an injunction against the enforcement of the federal statute. A federal district court denied the motion but, on appeal before a three-judge panel, the U.S. Court of Appeals for the Ninth Circuit reversed that decision, holding that, based on rulings in *United States v. Lopez*, 514 U.S. 549 (1995) (excerpted in Vol. 1, Ch. 6) and *United States v. Morrison*, 529 U.S. 598 (2000) (excerpted in Vol. 1, Ch. 6), the application of the CSA to Raich and Monson exceeded Congress's regulatory power under the Commerce Clause, and rejected the government's argument that the "aggregation principle" upheld in *Wickard v. Filburn*, 317 U.S. 111 (1942) (excerpted in Vol. 1, Ch. 6), applied, ruling instead that the principle was inapplicable to the activities of Raich and Monson. The Department of Justice appealed that decision and the Supreme Court granted review.

The appellate court's decision was reversed on a vote of six to three. Justice Stevens delivered the opinion of the Court and Justice Scalia filed a concurring opinion. Chief Justice Rehnquist and Justices O'Connor and Thomas dissented.

□ *Justice STEVENS delivered the opinion of the Court.*

California is one of at least nine States that authorize the use of marijuana for medicinal purposes. The question presented in this case is whether the power vested in Congress by Article I, Section 8, of the Constitution "[t]o make all Laws which shall be necessary and proper for carrying into Execution" its authority to "regulate Commerce with foreign Nations, and among the several States" includes the power to prohibit the local cultivation and use of marijuana in compliance with California law. . . .

The obvious importance of the case prompted our grant of *certiorari*. The case is made difficult by respondents' strong arguments that they will suffer irreparable harm because, despite a congressional finding to the contrary, marijuana does have valid therapeutic purposes. The question before us, however, is not whether it is wise to enforce the statute in these circumstances; rather, it is whether Congress's power to regulate interstate markets for medicinal substances encompasses the portions of those markets that are supplied with drugs produced and consumed locally. Well-settled law controls our answer. The CSA is a valid exercise of federal power, even as applied to the troubling facts of this case. We accordingly vacate the judgment of the Court of Appeals.

Shortly after taking office in 1969, President Nixon declared a national "war on drugs." As the first campaign of that war, Congress set out to enact legislation that would consolidate various drug laws on the books into a comprehensive statute, provide meaningful regulation over legitimate sources of drugs to prevent diversion into illegal channels, and strengthen law enforcement tools against the traffic in illicit drugs. That effort culminated in the passage of the Comprehensive Drug Abuse Prevention and Control Act of 1970. . . .

In enacting the CSA, Congress classified marijuana as a Schedule I drug. This preliminary classification was based, in part, on the recommendation of the Assistant Secretary of HEW "that marihuana be retained within schedule I at least until the completion of certain studies now underway." Schedule I drugs are categorized as such because of their high potential for abuse, lack of any accepted medical use, and absence of any accepted safety for use in medically supervised treatment. . . .

Respondents in this case do not dispute that passage of the CSA, as part of the Comprehensive Drug Abuse Prevention and Control Act, was well within Congress's commerce power. Nor do they contend that any provision or section of the CSA amounts to an unconstitutional exercise of congressional authority. Rather, respondents' challenge is actually quite limited; they argue that the CSA's categorical prohibition of the manufacture and possession of marijuana as applied to the intrastate manufacture and possession of marijuana for medical purposes pursuant to California law exceeds Congress's authority under the Commerce Clause.

In assessing the validity of congressional regulation, none of our Commerce Clause cases can be viewed in isolation. As charted in considerable detail in *United States v. Lopez*, [514 U.S. 549 (1995)], our understanding of the reach of the Commerce Clause, as well as Congress's assertion of authority thereunder, has evolved over time. The Commerce Clause emerged as the Framers' response to the central problem giving rise to the Constitution itself: the absence of any federal commerce power under the Articles of Confederation. For the first century of our history, the primary use of the Clause was to preclude the kind of discriminatory state legislation that had once been permissible. Then, in response to rapid industrial development and an increasingly interdependent national economy, Congress "ushered in a new era of federal regulation under the commerce power," beginning with the enactment of the Interstate Commerce Act in 1887, and the Sherman Antitrust Act in 1890. Cases decided during that "new era," which now spans more than a century, have identified three general categories of regulation in which Congress is authorized to engage under its commerce power. First, Congress can regulate the channels of interstate commerce. *Perez v. United States*, 402 U.S. 146 (1971). Second, Congress has authority to regulate and protect the instrumentalities of interstate commerce, and persons or things in interstate commerce. Third, Congress has the power to regulate activities that substantially affect interstate commerce. *NLRB v. Jones & Laughlin Steel Corp.*, 301 U.S. 1 (1937). Only the third category is implicated in the case at hand.

Our case law firmly establishes Congress's power to regulate purely local activities that are part of an economic "class of activities" that have a substantial effect on interstate commerce. See, e.g., *Perez*; *Wickard v. Filburn*, 317 U.S. 111 (1942). As we stated in *Wickard*, "even if appellee's activity be local and though it may not be regarded as commerce, it may still, whatever its nature, be reached by Congress if it exerts a substantial economic effect on interstate commerce." We have never required Congress to legislate with scientific exactitude. When Congress decides that the "'total incidence'" of a practice poses a threat to a national market, it may regulate the entire class. In this vein, we have reiterated that when "'a general regulatory statute bears a substantial relation to commerce, the *de minimis* character of individual instances arising under that statute is of no consequence.'"

Our decision in *Wickard* is of particular relevance. In *Wickard*, we upheld the application of regulations promulgated under the Agricultural Adjustment Act of 1938, which were designed to control the volume of wheat moving in interstate and foreign commerce in order to avoid surpluses and consequent abnormally low prices. The regulations established an allotment of 11.1 acres for Filburn's 1941 wheat crop, but he sowed 23 acres, intending to use the excess by consuming it on his own farm. Filburn argued that even though we had sustained Congress's power to regulate the production of goods for commerce, that power did not authorize "federal regulation [of] production not intended in any part for commerce but wholly for consumption on the farm." Justice JACKSON's opinion for a unanimous Court rejected this submission. *Wickard* thus establishes that Congress can regulate purely intrastate activity that is not itself "commercial," in that it is not produced for sale, if it concludes that failure to regulate that class of activity would undercut the regulation of the interstate market in that commodity.

The similarities between this case and *Wickard* are striking. Like the farmer in *Wickard*, respondents are cultivating, for home consumption, a fungible commodity for which there is an established, albeit illegal, interstate market. Just as the Agricultural Adjustment Act was designed "to control the volume [of wheat] moving in interstate and foreign commerce in order to avoid surpluses . . ." and consequently control the market price, a primary purpose of the CSA is to control the supply and demand of controlled substances in both lawful and unlawful drug markets. In *Wickard*, we had no difficulty concluding that Congress had a rational basis for believing that, when viewed in the aggregate, leaving home-consumed wheat outside the regulatory scheme would have a substantial influence on price and market conditions. Here too, Congress had a rational basis for concluding that leaving home-consumed marijuana outside federal control would similarly affect price and market conditions.

More concretely, one concern prompting inclusion of wheat grown for home consumption in the 1938 Act was that rising market prices could draw such wheat into the interstate market, resulting in lower market prices. The parallel concern making it appropriate to include marijuana grown for home consumption in the CSA is the likelihood that the high demand in the interstate market will draw such marijuana into that market. While the diversion of homegrown wheat tended to frustrate the federal interest in stabilizing prices by regulating the volume of commercial transactions in the interstate market, the diversion of homegrown marijuana tends to frustrate the federal interest in eliminating commercial transactions in the interstate market in their entirety. In both cases, the regulation is squarely within Congress's commerce power because production of the commodity meant for home consumption, be it wheat or marijuana, has a substantial effect on supply and demand in the national market for that commodity.

Nonetheless, respondents suggest that *Wickard* differs from this case in three respects: (1) the Agricultural Adjustment Act, unlike the CSA, exempted small farming operations; (2) *Wickard* involved a "quintessential economic activity"—a commercial farm—whereas respondents do not sell marijuana; and (3) the *Wickard* record made it clear that the aggregate production of wheat for use on farms had a significant impact on market prices. Those differences, though factually accurate, do not diminish the precedential force of this Court's reasoning.

The fact that Wickard's own impact on the market was "trivial by itself" was not a sufficient reason for removing him from the scope of federal regulation. That the Secretary of Agriculture elected to exempt even smaller farms from regulation does not speak to his power to regulate all those whose aggregated production was significant, nor did that fact play any role in the Court's analysis. Moreover, even though Wickard was indeed a commercial farmer, the activity he was engaged in—the cultivation of wheat for home consumption—was not treated by the Court as part of his commercial farming operation. And while it is true that the record in the *Wickard* case itself established the causal connection between the production for local use and the national market, we have before us findings by Congress to the same effect. . . .

In assessing the scope of Congress's authority under the Commerce Clause, we stress that the task before us is a modest one. We need not determine whether respondents' activities, taken in the aggregate, substantially affect interstate commerce in fact, but only whether a "rational basis" exists for so concluding.

Given the enforcement difficulties that attend distinguishing between marijuana cultivated locally and marijuana grown elsewhere, and concerns about diversion into illicit channels, we have no difficulty concluding that Congress had a rational basis for believing that failure to regulate the intrastate manufacture and possession of marijuana would leave a gaping hole in the CSA. Thus, as in *Wickard*, when it enacted comprehensive legislation to regulate the interstate market in a fungible commodity, Congress was acting well within its authority to "make all Laws which shall be necessary and proper" to "regulate Commerce . . . among the several States." That the regulation ensnares some purely intrastate activity is of no moment. As we have done many times before, we refuse to excise individual components of that larger scheme.

To support their contrary submission, respondents rely heavily on two of our more recent Commerce Clause cases. In their myopic focus, they overlook the larger context of modern-era Commerce Clause jurisprudence preserved by those cases. Moreover, even in the narrow prism of respondents' creation, they read those cases far too broadly. Those two cases, of course, are *Lopez* and [*United States v.*] *Morrison*, 529 U.S. 598 [(2000)]. As an initial matter, the statutory challenges at issue in those cases were markedly different from the challenge respondents pursue in the case at hand. Here, respondents ask us to excise individual applications of a concededly valid statutory scheme. In contrast, in both *Lopez* and *Morrison*, the parties asserted that a particular statute or provision fell outside Congress's commerce power in its entirety. This distinction is pivotal for we have often reiterated that "[w]here the class of activities is regulated and that class is within the reach of federal power, the courts have no power 'to excise, as trivial, individual instances' of the class." *Perez*. . . .

Unlike those at issue in *Lopez* and *Morrison*, the activities regulated by the CSA are quintessentially economic. "Economics" refers to "the production, distribution, and consumption of commodities." The CSA is a statute that regulates the production, distribution, and consumption of commodities for which there is an established, and lucrative, interstate market. Prohibiting the intrastate possession or manufacture of an article of commerce is a rational (and commonly utilized) means of regulating commerce in that product. Such prohibitions include specific decisions requiring that a drug be withdrawn from the market as a result of the failure to comply with regulatory requirements as well as decisions excluding Schedule I drugs entirely from the market. Because the CSA is a statute that directly regulates economic, commercial activity, our opinion in *Morrison* casts no doubt on its constitutionality.

The Court of Appeals was able to conclude otherwise only by isolating a "separate and distinct" class of activities that it held to be beyond the reach of federal power, defined as "the intrastate, noncommercial cultivation, possession and use of marijuana for personal medical purposes on the advice of a physician and in accordance with state law." The court characterized this class as "different in kind from drug trafficking." The differences between the members of a class so defined and the principal traffickers in Schedule I substances might be sufficient to justify a policy decision exempting the narrower class from the coverage of the CSA. The question, however, is whether Congress's contrary policy judgment, i.e., its decision to include this narrower "class of activities" within the larger regulatory scheme, was constitutionally deficient. We have no difficulty concluding that Congress acted rationally in determining that none of the characteristics making up the purported class, whether viewed individually or in the aggregate, compelled an exemption from the CSA; rather, the subdivided class of activities defined by the Court of Appeals was an essential part of the larger regulatory scheme.

First, the fact that marijuana is used "for personal medical purposes on the advice of a physician" cannot itself serve as a distinguishing factor. The

CSA designates marijuana as contraband for any purpose; in fact, by characterizing marijuana as a Schedule I drug, Congress expressly found that the drug has no acceptable medical uses. . . .

Second, limiting the activity to marijuana possession and cultivation "in accordance with state law" cannot serve to place respondents' activities beyond congressional reach. The Supremacy Clause unambiguously provides that if there is any conflict between federal and state law, federal law shall prevail. It is beyond peradventure that federal power over commerce is " 'superior to that of the States to provide for the welfare or necessities of their inhabitants,' " however legitimate or dire those necessities may be. Just as state acquiescence to federal regulation cannot expand the bounds of the Commerce Clause, so too state action cannot circumscribe Congress's plenary commerce power.

So, from the "separate and distinct" class of activities identified by the Court of Appeals (and adopted by the dissenters), we are left with "the intrastate, noncommercial cultivation, possession and use of marijuana." Thus the case for the exemption comes down to the claim that a locally cultivated product that is used domestically rather than sold on the open market is not subject to federal regulation. Given the findings in the CSA and the undisputed magnitude of the commercial market for marijuana, our decisions in *Wickard v. Filburn* and the later cases endorsing its reasoning foreclose that claim. . . .

□ *Justice SCALIA, concurring in the judgment.*

I write separately because my understanding of the doctrinal foundation on which that holding rests is, if not inconsistent with that of the Court, at least more nuanced.

Since *Perez v. United States*, 402 U.S. 146 (1971), our cases have mechanically recited that the Commerce Clause permits congressional regulation of three categories: (1) the channels of interstate commerce; (2) the instrumentalities of interstate commerce, and persons or things in interstate commerce; and (3) activities that "substantially affect" interstate commerce. The first two categories are self-evident, since they are the ingredients of interstate commerce itself. See *Gibbons v. Ogden*, 9 Wheat. 1 (1824). The third category, however, is different in kind, and its recitation without explanation is misleading and incomplete.

It is misleading because, unlike the channels, instrumentalities, and agents of interstate commerce, activities that substantially affect interstate commerce are not themselves part of interstate commerce, and thus the power to regulate them cannot come from the Commerce Clause alone. Rather, as this Court has acknowledged since at least *United States v. Coombs*, 12 Pet. 72 (1838), Congress's regulatory authority over intrastate activities that are not themselves part of interstate commerce (including activities that have a substantial effect on interstate commerce) derives from the Necessary and Proper Clause. And the category of "activities that substantially affect interstate commerce" is incomplete because the authority to enact laws necessary and proper for the regulation of interstate commerce is not limited to laws governing intrastate activities that substantially affect interstate commerce. Where necessary to make a regulation of interstate commerce effective, Congress may regulate even those intrastate activities that do not themselves substantially affect interstate commerce.

Our cases show that the regulation of intrastate activities may be necessary to and proper for the regulation of interstate commerce in two general circumstances. Most directly, the commerce power permits Congress not only to devise rules for the governance of commerce between States but also to facilitate interstate commerce by eliminating potential obstructions, and to restrict it by eliminating potential stimulants. See *NLRB v. Jones & Laughlin Steel Corp.*, 301 U.S. 1 (1937). That is why the Court has repeatedly sustained congressional legislation on the ground that the regulated activities had a substantial effect on interstate commerce. *Lopez* and *Morrison* recognized the expansive scope of Congress's authority in this regard: "[T]he pattern is clear. Where economic activity substantially affects interstate commerce, legislation regulating that activity will be sustained." *Lopez*.

This principle is not without limitation. In *Lopez* and *Morrison*, the Court—conscious of the potential of the "substantially affects" test to " 'obliterate the distinction between what is national and what is local,' "—rejected the argument that Congress may regulate noneconomic activity based solely on the effect that it may have on interstate commerce through a remote chain of inferences. Thus, although Congress's authority to regulate intrastate activity that substantially affects interstate commerce is broad, it does not permit the Court to "pile inference upon inference" in order to establish that noneconomic activity has a substantial effect on interstate commerce. As we implicitly acknowledged in *Lopez*, however, Congress's authority to enact laws necessary and proper for the regulation of interstate commerce is not limited to laws directed against economic activities that have a substantial effect on interstate commerce. Though the conduct in *Lopez* was not economic, the Court nevertheless recognized that it could be regulated as "an essential part of a larger regulation of economic activity, in which the regulatory scheme could be undercut unless the intrastate activity were regulated." This statement referred to those cases permitting the regulation of intrastate activities "which in a substantial way interfere with or obstruct the exercise of the granted power."

Although this power "to make . . . regulation effective" commonly overlaps with the authority to regulate economic activities that substantially affect interstate commerce, and may in some cases have been confused with that authority, the two are distinct. The regulation of an intrastate activity may be essential to a comprehensive regulation of interstate commerce even though the intrastate activity does not itself "substantially affect" interstate commerce. Moreover, as the passage from *Lopez* quoted above suggests, Congress may regulate even noneconomic local activity if that regulation is a necessary part of a more general regulation of interstate commerce. The relevant question is simply whether the means chosen are "reasonably adapted" to the attainment of a legitimate end under the commerce power. . . .

As the Court said in the *Shreveport Rate Cases*, [234 U.S. 342 (1914)], the Necessary and Proper Clause does not give "Congress . . . the authority to regulate the internal commerce of a State, as such," but it does allow Congress "to take all measures necessary or appropriate to" the effective regulation of the interstate market, "although intrastate transactions . . . may thereby be controlled."

Today's principal dissent objects that, by permitting Congress to regulate activities necessary to effective interstate regulation, the Court reduces *Lopez* and *Morrison* to "little more than a drafting guide." (CONNOR, J.). I think that criticism unjustified. Unlike the power to regulate activities that have a substantial effect on interstate commerce, the power to enact laws enabling effective regulation of interstate commerce can only be exercised in conjunction with congressional regulation of an interstate market, and it extends only to those measures necessary to make the interstate regulation effective. As *Lopez* itself states, and the Court affirms today, Congress may regulate noneconomic intrastate activities only where the failure to do so "could . . . undercut" its regulation of interstate commerce. This is not a power that threatens to obliterate the line between "what is truly national and what is truly local." . . .

Lopez and *Morrison* affirm that Congress may not regulate certain "purely local" activity within the States based solely on the attenuated effect that such activity may have in the interstate market. But those decisions do not declare noneconomic intrastate activities to be categorically beyond the reach of the Federal Government. Neither case involved the power of Congress to exert control over intrastate activities in connection with a more comprehensive scheme of regulation. . . .

The application of these principles to the case before us is straightforward. In the CSA, Congress has undertaken to extinguish the interstate market in Schedule I controlled substances, including marijuana. The Commerce Clause unquestionably permits this. The power to regulate interstate commerce "extends not only to those regulations which aid, foster and protect the commerce, but embraces those which prohibit it." To effectuate its objective, Congress has prohibited almost all intrastate activities related to Schedule I substances—both economic activities (manufacture, distribution, possession with the intent to distribute) and noneconomic activities (simple possession). That simple possession is a noneconomic activity is immaterial to whether it can be prohibited as a necessary part of a larger regulation. Rather, Congress's authority to enact all of these prohibitions of intrastate controlled-substance activities depends only upon whether they are appropriate means of achieving the legitimate end of eradicating Schedule I substances from interstate commerce.

By this measure, I think the regulation must be sustained. . . .

□ *Justice O'CONNOR, with whom THE CHIEF JUSTICE and Justice THOMAS join as to all but Part III, dissenting.*

We enforce the "outer limits" of Congress's Commerce Clause authority not for their own sake, but to protect historic spheres of state sovereignty from excessive federal encroachment and thereby to maintain the distribution of power fundamental to our federalist system of government. One of federalism's chief virtues, of course, is that it promotes innovation by allowing for the possibility that "a single courageous State may, if its citizens choose, serve as a laboratory; and try novel social and economic experiments without risk to the rest of the country." *New State Ice Co. v. Liebmann*, 285 U.S. 262 (1932) (BRANDEIS, J., dissenting).

This case exemplifies the role of States as laboratories. The States' core police powers have always included authority to define criminal law and to protect the health, safety, and welfare of their citizens. Exercising those powers, California (by ballot initiative and then by legislative codification) has come to its own conclusion about the difficult and sensitive question of whether marijuana should be available to relieve severe pain and suffering.

Today the Court sanctions an application of the federal Controlled Substances Act that extinguishes that experiment, without any proof that the personal cultivation, possession, and use of marijuana for medicinal purposes, if economic activity in the first place, has a substantial effect on interstate commerce and is therefore an appropriate subject of federal regulation. In so doing, the Court announces a rule that gives Congress a perverse incentive to legislate broadly pursuant to the Commerce Clause—nestling questionable assertions of its authority into comprehensive regulatory schemes—rather than with precision. That rule and the result it produces in this case are irreconcilable with our decisions in *Lopez* and *United States v. Morrison*, 529 U.S. 598 (2000). Accordingly I dissent.

Our decision [in *Lopez*] about whether gun possession in school zones substantially affected interstate commerce turned on four considerations. First, we observed that our "substantial effects" cases generally have upheld federal regulation of economic activity that affected interstate commerce, but that Section 922(q) was a criminal statute having "nothing to do with 'commerce' or any sort of economic enterprise." Second, we noted that the statute contained no express jurisdictional requirement establishing its connection to interstate commerce.

Third, we found telling the absence of legislative findings about the regulated conduct's impact on interstate commerce. We explained that while express legislative findings are neither required nor, when provided, dispositive, findings "enable us to evaluate the legislative judgment that the activity in question substantially affect[s] interstate commerce, even though no such substantial effect [is] visible to the naked eye." Finally, we rejected as too attenuated the Government's argument that firearm possession in school zones could result in violent crime which in turn could adversely affect the national economy. The Constitution, we said, does not tolerate reasoning that would "convert congressional authority under the Commerce Clause to a general police power of the sort retained by the States." Later in *Morrison*, we relied on the same four considerations to hold that Section 40302 of the Violence Against Women Act of 1994 exceeded Congress's authority under the Commerce Clause.

In my view, the case before us is materially indistinguishable from *Lopez* and *Morrison* when the same considerations are taken into account. . . .

Today's decision allows Congress to regulate intrastate activity without check, so long as there is some implication by legislative design that regulating intrastate activity is essential (and the Court appears to equate "essential" with "necessary") to the interstate regulatory scheme. Seizing upon our language in *Lopez* that the statute prohibiting gun possession in school zones was "not an essential part of a larger regulation of economic activity, in which the regulatory scheme could be undercut unless the intrastate activity were regulated," the Court appears to reason that the placement of local activity in a comprehensive scheme confirms that it is essential to that scheme. If the Court is right, then *Lopez* stands for nothing more than a drafting guide: Congress should have described the relevant crime as "transfer or possession of a firearm anywhere in the nation"—thus including commercial and noncommercial activity, and clearly encompassing some activity with assuredly substantial effect on interstate commerce. Had it done so, the majority hints, we would have sustained its authority to regulate possession of firearms in school zones. Furthermore, today's decision suggests we would readily sustain a congressional decision to attach the regulation of intrastate activity to a preexisting comprehensive (or even not-so-comprehensive) scheme. If so, the Court invites increased federal regulation of local activity even if, as it suggests, Congress would not enact a new interstate scheme exclusively for the sake of reaching intrastate activity.

I cannot agree that our decision in *Lopez* contemplated such evasive or overbroad legislative strategies with approval. Until today, such arguments have been made only in dissent. *Lopez* and *Morrison* did not indicate that the constitutionality of federal regulation depends on superficial and formalistic distinctions. Likewise I did not understand our discussion of the role of courts in enforcing outer limits of the Commerce Clause for the sake of maintaining the federalist balance our Constitution requires, as a signal to Congress to enact legislation that is more extensive and more intrusive into the domain of state power. If the Court always defers to Congress as it does today, little may be left to the notion of enumerated powers.

The hard work for courts, then, is to identify objective markers for confining the analysis in Commerce Clause cases. . . . A number of objective markers are available to confine the scope of constitutional review here. Both federal and state legislation—including the CSA itself, the California Compassionate Use Act, and other state medical marijuana legislation—recognize that medical and nonmedical (i.e., recreational) uses of drugs are realistically distinct and can be segregated, and regulate them differently. Moreover, because fundamental structural concerns about dual sovereignty animate our Commerce Clause cases, it is relevant that this case involves the interplay of federal and state regulation in areas of criminal law and social policy, where "States lay claim by right of history and expertise." *Lopez*. California, like other States, has drawn on its reserved powers to distinguish the regulation of medicinal marijuana. To ascertain whether Congress's encroachment is constitutionally justified in this case, then, I would focus here on the personal cultivation, possession, and use of marijuana for medicinal purposes.

Having thus defined the relevant conduct, we must determine whether, under our precedents, the conduct is economic and, in the aggregate, substantially affects interstate commerce. Even if intrastate cultivation and possession of marijuana for one's own medicinal use can properly be characterized as economic, and I question whether it can, it has not been shown that such activity substantially affects interstate commerce. Similarly, it is neither self-evident nor demonstrated that regulating such activity is necessary to the interstate drug control scheme.

The Court's definition of economic activity is breathtaking. It defines as economic any activity involving the production, distribution, and consumption of commodities. And it appears to reason that when an interstate market for a commodity exists, regulating the intrastate manufacture or possession of that commodity is constitutional either because that intrastate activity is itself economic, or because regulating it is a rational part of regulating its market. Putting to one side the problem endemic to the Court's opinion—the shift in focus from the activity at issue in this case to the entirety of what the CSA regulates—the Court's definition of economic activity for purposes of Commerce Clause jurisprudence threatens to sweep all of productive human activity into federal regulatory reach. . . .

The Court suggests that *Wickard*, which we have identified as "perhaps the most far reaching example of Commerce Clause authority over intrastate activity," established federal regulatory power over any home consumption of a commodity for which a national market exists. I disagree. *Wickard* involved a challenge to the Agricultural Adjustment Act of 1938 (AAA), which directed the Secretary of Agriculture to set national quotas on wheat production, and penalties for excess production. The AAA itself confirmed that Congress made an explicit choice not to reach—and thus the Court could not possibly have approved of federal control over—small-scale, noncommercial wheat farming. . . .

Even assuming that economic activity is at issue in this case, the Government has made no showing in fact that the possession and use of homegrown marijuana for medical purposes, in California or elsewhere, has a substantial effect on interstate commerce. Similarly, the Government has not shown that regulating such activity is necessary to an interstate regulatory scheme. Whatever the specific theory of "substantial effects" at issue (i.e., whether the activity substantially affects interstate commerce, whether its regulation is necessary to an interstate regulatory scheme, or both), a concern for dual sovereignty requires that Congress's excursion into the traditional domain of States be justified.

That is why characterizing this as a case about the Necessary and Proper Clause does not change the analysis significantly. Congress must exercise its authority under the Necessary and Proper Clause in a manner consistent with basic constitutional principles. Congress cannot use its authority under the Clause to contravene the principle of state sovereignty embodied in the Tenth Amendment. Likewise, that authority must be used in a manner consistent with the notion of enumerated powers—a structural principle that is as much part of the Constitution as the Tenth Amendment's explicit textual command. Accordingly, something more than mere assertion is required when Congress purports to have power over local activity whose connection to an intrastate market is not self-evident. Otherwise, the Necessary and Proper Clause will always be a back door for unconstitutional federal regulation. Cf. *Printz v. United States*, 521 U.S. 898 (1997) (the Necessary and Proper Clause is "the last, best hope of those who defend *ultra vires* congressional action"). . . .

There is simply no evidence that homegrown medicinal marijuana users constitute, in the aggregate, a sizable enough class to have a discernable, let alone substantial, impact on the national illicit drug market—or otherwise to threaten the CSA regime. Explicit evidence is helpful when substantial effect is not "visible to the naked eye." And here, in part because common sense suggests that medical marijuana users may be limited in number and that California's Compassionate Use Act and similar state legislation may well isolate activities relating to medicinal marijuana from the illicit market, the effect of those activities on interstate drug traffic is not self-evidently substantial. . . .

Relying on Congress's abstract assertions, the Court has endorsed making it a federal crime to grow small amounts of marijuana in one's own home for one's own medicinal use. This overreaching stifles an express choice by some States, concerned for the lives and liberties of their people, to regulate medical marijuana differently. If I were a California citizen, I would not have voted for the medical marijuana ballot initiative; if I were a California legislator I would not have supported the Compassionate Use Act. But whatever the wisdom of California's experiment with medical marijuana, the federalism principles that have driven our Commerce Clause cases require that room for experiment be protected in this case. For these reasons I dissent.

□ *Justice THOMAS, dissenting.*

As I explained at length in *United States v. Lopez*, 514 U.S. 549 (1995), the Commerce Clause empowers Congress to regulate the buying and selling of goods and services trafficked across state lines. The Clause's text, structure, and history all indicate that, at the time of the founding, the term " 'commerce' consisted of selling, buying, and bartering, as well as transporting for these purposes." Commerce, or trade, stood in contrast to productive activities like manufacturing and agriculture. Throughout founding-era dictionaries, Madison's notes from the Constitutional Convention, *The Federalist Papers*, and the ratification debates, the term "commerce" is consistently used to mean trade or exchange—not all economic or gainful activity that has some attenuated connection to trade or exchange. The term "commerce" commonly meant trade or exchange (and shipping for these purposes) not simply to those involved in the drafting and ratification processes, but also to the general public.

Even the majority does not argue that respondents' conduct is itself "Commerce among the several States." Monson and Raich neither buy nor sell the marijuana that they consume. They cultivate their cannabis entirely in the State of California—it never crosses state lines, much less as part of a commercial transaction. Certainly no evidence from the founding suggests that "commerce" included the mere possession of a good or some purely personal activity that did not involve trade or exchange for value. In the early days of the Republic, it would have been unthinkable that Congress could prohibit the local cultivation, possession, and consumption of marijuana.

On this traditional understanding of "commerce," the Controlled Substances Act (CSA) regulates a great deal of marijuana trafficking that is interstate and commercial in character. The CSA does not, however, criminalize only the interstate buying and selling of marijuana. Instead, it bans the entire market—intrastate or interstate, noncommercial or commercial—for marijuana. Respondents are correct that the CSA exceeds Congress's commerce power as applied to their conduct, which is purely intrastate and noncommercial. . . .

The majority prevents States like California from devising drug policies that they have concluded provide much-needed respite to the seriously ill. It does so without any serious inquiry into the necessity for federal regulation or the propriety of "displac[ing] state regulation in areas of traditional state concern." Our federalist system, properly understood, allows California and a growing number of other States to decide for themselves how to safeguard the health and welfare of their citizens. I would affirm the judgment of the Court of Appeals. I respectfully dissent.

7

The States and American Federalism

A | *States' Power over Commerce and Regulation*

■ The Development of Law

Other Rulings on State Regulatory Powers in Alleged Conflict with Federal Legislation

CASE	RULING
Bates v. Dow Agrosciences, 125 S.Ct. 1788 (2005)	Writing for the Court, Justice Stevens held that the Federal Insecticide Fungicide and Rodenticide Act (FIFRA) does not preempt state laws and tort relief lawsuits in state courts against manufacturers for negligently designed and manufactured products. Because the FIFRA does not provide for suits in federal courts, the ruling was significant since a contrary ruling would have denied consumers any opportunity to sue manufacturers. However, Justice Stevens also emphasized that not all state lawsuits under federal statutes are permitted. Preemption of each federal statute must be determined in light of its own statutory language, legislative history, and the history of litigation over a regulated product. Justices Scalia and Thomas dissented.

Mid-Con Freight Systems, Inc. v. Michigan Public Service Commission, 125 S.Ct. 2427 (2005)

Federal law requires interstate truckers to obtain a federal permit and by 1991 some 39 states also demanded such proof. Because of differences in the states, Congress created a Single State Registration System (SSRS), which allows companies to file one set of state and federal registration forms, and prohibits states from imposing additional registration fees. Michigan imposed an annual $100 fee for state-licensed trucks and its law was challenged. Writing for the Court, Justice Breyer held that the federal law did not preempt Michigan's law because the federal statute only applies to the SSRS registration and does not preclude additional state regulations. Justice Kennedy, joined by Chief Justice Rehnquist and Justice O'Connor, dissented.

■ The Development of Law

Other Rulings on State Regulation of Commerce in the Absence of Federal Legislation

CASE

RULING

Granholm v. Heald, 125 S.Ct. 1885 (2005)

A bare majority struck down Michigan and New York laws that forbid wineries located out of state from shipping wine directly to consumers. The ruling will have wide-ranging consequences for alcohol sales on the Internet and affect laws in 18 other states. Writing for the Court, Justice Kennedy noted that there was a "patchwork of laws," with some states banning all direct shipments, others only out-of-state shipments, and some requiring reciprocity. That amounted to "an ongoing, low-level trade war" that discriminated against interstate commerce. Such discrimination, Justice Kennedy ruled, was "neither authorized nor permitted by the Twenty-first Amendment," which gives states the authority to regulate the importation of liquor. In reversing the lower courts, Justice Kennedy emphasized that the Twenty-first Amendment "should not be subordinated to the dormant Commerce Clause," and noted that numerous previous decisions had rejected the "argument that the Twenty-first Amendment has somehow operated to 'repeal' the Commerce Clause for alcoholic beverages." In sum, "in all but the narrowest circumstances, state laws violate the Commerce Clause if they mandate differential treatment of in-state and out-of-state economic interests that benefits the former and burdens the later." Justices Stevens and Thomas issued dissenting opinions, which Chief Justice Rehnquist and Justice O'Connor joined.

American Trucking Associations, Inc. v. Michigan Public Service Commission, 125 S.Ct. 2419 (2005)

Writing for the Court, Justice Breyer ruled that the dormant Commerce Clause does not preclude Michigan from imposing a $100 annual fee on trucks engaged in intrastate commercial hauling, and does not discriminate against interstate commerce. Justices Scalia and Thomas filed concurring opinions.

8

Representative Government, Voting Rights, and Electoral Politics

C | *Campaigns and Elections*

■ The Development of Law

Other Rulings on Campaigns and Elections

CASE	VOTE	RULING
Clingman v. Beaver, 125 S.Ct. 2029 (2005)	6:3	Writing for the Court, Justice Thomas upheld Oklahoma's semiclosed primary law, under which political parties may permit only their own registered members and voters registered as independents to vote in a primary. The Libertarian Party had wanted to open its primary to members of other parties and challenged the law for infringing on its First Amendment freedom of association. But Justice Thomas held that the law imposed only minor burdens and advanced the state's compelling interests in preserving political parties "as viable and identifiable interest groups." Justices Stevens, O'Connor, and Souter dissented.

9

ECONOMIC RIGHTS AND AMERICAN CAPITALISM

C | *The "Takings Clause" and Just Compensation*

In a major ruling with wide-ranging ramifications for urban planners and homeowners, by a five to four vote the Court upheld the use of the government's power of eminent domain and to condemn and take, with just compensation, private property for the purpose of advancing the economic development of the community. Writing for the Court in *Kelo v. City of New London* (excerpted below), Justice Stevens held that "public use" was not limited to the use of public domain to build a road or a bridge; or to develop a blighted neighborhood, as in *Berman v. Parker*, 348 U.S. 26 (1954); or to redistribute land ownership, as in *Hawaii Housing Authority v. Midkiff*, 467 U.S. 229 (1984) (excerpted in Vol. 1, Ch. 9, and in Vol. 2, Ch. 3); but includes "promoting economic development," even if the property was taken and sold for development by private developers. Justice Stevens emphasized that courts should be deferential to the decisions of state and local authorities. Justice Kennedy cast the pivotal fifth vote and filed a concurring opinion, underscoring that courts should still exercise review in such cases in order to ensure that governments do not use their power of eminent domain to simply reward or advance the interests of businesses and powerful private interests. Justice O'Connor filed a dissenting opinion, which was joined by Chief Justice Rehnquist, and Justices Scalia and Thomas dissented. Justice Thomas also filed a dissenting opinion, criticizing the majority for departing from the "original intent" of the Fifth Amendment and warning that the decision would have an adverse impact on the poor and minorities living in inner cities, whose property could be condemned by the government and then sold to private developers.

Kelo v. City of New London, Connecticut

125 S.Ct. 2655 (2005)

The city of New London is at the junction of the Thames River and Long Island Sound in southeastern Connecticut. Decades of economic decline led the state in 1990 to designate the city a "distressed municipality." In 1996, the federal government closed the Naval Undersea Warfare Center, which had been located in the Fort Trumbull area of the city and had employed over 1,500 people. In 1998, the city's unemployment rate was nearly double that of the state, and its population of just under 24,000 residents was at its lowest since 1920. These conditions prompted state and local officials to target New London, and particularly its Fort Trumbull area, for economic revitalization. The New London Development Corporation (NLDC), a private nonprofit entity, was authorized to assist the city in planning economic development. In January 1998, Connecticut approved a $5.35 million bond issue to support the NLDC's planning activities and a $10 million bond issue for the creation of a Fort Trumbull State Park. In February, the pharmaceutical company Pfizer announced that it would build a $300 million research facility in the Fort Trumbull area, and the NLDC hoped that that would draw new business to the area. The Fort Trumbull area is on a peninsula that juts into the Thames River and includes approximately 115 privately owned properties, as well as the 32 acres of land formerly occupied by the naval facility. The NLDC's development plan called for the creation of a waterfront conference hotel at the center of a "small urban village," including restaurants and stores, as well as a pedestrian "riverwalk" that would continue down the coast, along with a new U.S. Coast Guard Museum, a renovated marina, and research and development office space. The NLDC's development plan aimed to capitalize on the arrival of the Pfizer facility and the new commerce it would attract. In addition to creating jobs and generating tax revenue, the plan sought to create recreational opportunities on the waterfront and in the park. The city council approved the plan in January 2000, and designated the NLDC its development agent. The city council also authorized the NLDC to purchase property or to acquire property by exercising eminent domain in the city's name. The NLDC successfully negotiated the purchase of most of the real estate in the 90-acre area, but its negotiations with some homeowners failed and the NLDC initiated the condemnation proceedings against them.

Susette Kelo lived in the Fort Trumbull area and had made extensive improvements to her well-maintained house, which overlooks the Thames River. In December 2000, Kelo and a few other homeowners of condemned property sued New London, claiming that the taking of their properties, even with just compensation, violated the "public use" restriction in the Fifth Amendment, because their properties would not be used for a public purpose, like building a road, but instead sold to private parties for development—development that the city claimed would economically benefit the community. A trial court granted a restraining order prohibiting New London's taking of some of the properties, but on appeal the state supreme court ruled that the city could take all of the properties. Kelo appealed that decision and the Supreme Court granted review.

The state supreme court's decision was affirmed by a five to four vote. Justice Stevens delivered the opinion of the Court. Justice Kennedy filed a concurring opinion. Justice O'Connor, joined by Chief Justice Rehnquist and Justices Scalia and Thomas, dissented. Justice Thomas also filed a dissenting opinion.

□ *Justice STEVENS delivered the opinion of the Court.*

We granted *certiorari* to determine whether a city's decision to take property for the purpose of economic development satisfies the "public use" requirement of the Fifth Amendment. Two polar propositions are perfectly clear. On the one hand, it has long been accepted that the sovereign may not take the property of A for the sole purpose of transferring it to another private party B, even though A is paid just compensation. On the other hand, it is equally clear that a State may transfer property from one private party to another if future "use by the public" is the purpose of the taking; the condemnation of land for a railroad with common-carrier duties is a familiar example. Neither of these propositions, however, determines the disposition of this case.

As for the first proposition, the City would no doubt be forbidden from taking petitioners' land for the purpose of conferring a private benefit on a particular private party. See [*Hawaii Housing Authority v.*] *Midkiff*, 467 U.S. [229 (1984)] ("A purely private taking could not withstand the scrutiny of the public use requirement; it would serve no legitimate purpose of government and would thus be void"). Nor would the City be allowed to take property under the mere pretext of a public purpose, when its actual purpose was to bestow a private benefit. The takings before us, however, would be executed pursuant to a "carefully considered" development plan. The trial judge and all the members of the Supreme Court of Connecticut agreed that there was no evidence of an illegitimate purpose in this case. Therefore, as was true of the statute challenged in *Midkiff*, the City's development plan was not adopted "to benefit a particular class of identifiable individuals."

On the other hand, this is not a case in which the City is planning to open the condemned land—at least not in its entirety—to use by the general public. Nor will the private lessees of the land in any sense be required to operate like common carriers, making their services available to all comers. But although such a projected use would be sufficient to satisfy the public use requirement, this "Court long ago rejected any literal requirement that condemned property be put into use for the general public." Indeed, while many state courts in the mid-19th century endorsed "use by the public" as the proper definition of public use, that narrow view steadily eroded over time. Not only was the "use by the public" test difficult to administer (e.g., what proportion of the public need have access to the property? at what price?), but it proved to be impractical given the diverse and always evolving needs of society. Accordingly, when this Court began applying the Fifth Amendment to the States at the close of the 19th century, it embraced the broader and more natural interpretation of public use as "public purpose." Thus, in a case upholding a mining company's use of an aerial bucket line to transport ore over property it did not own, Justice HOLMES' opinion for the Court stressed "the inadequacy of use by the general public as a universal test." *Strickley v. Highland Boy Gold Mining Co.*, 200 U.S. 527 (1906). We have repeatedly and consistently rejected that narrow test ever since.

The disposition of this case therefore turns on the question whether the City's development plan serves a "public purpose." Without exception, our cases have defined that concept broadly, reflecting our longstanding policy of deference to legislative judgments in this field.

In *Berman v. Parker*, 348 U.S. 26 (1954), this Court upheld a redevelopment plan targeting a blighted area of Washington, D.C., in which most of the housing for the area's 5,000 inhabitants was beyond repair. Under the plan, the area would be condemned and part of it utilized for the construction of streets, schools, and other public facilities. The remainder of the land would be leased or sold to private parties for the purpose of redevelopment, including the construction of low-cost housing.

The owner of a department store located in the area challenged the condemnation, pointing out that his store was not itself blighted and arguing that the creation of a "better balanced, more attractive community" was not a valid public use. Writing for a unanimous Court, Justice DOUGLAS refused to evaluate this claim in isolation, deferring instead to the legislative and agency judgment that the area "must be planned as a whole" for the plan to be successful. The Court explained that "community redevelopment programs need not, by force of the Constitution, be on a piecemeal basis—lot by lot, building by building." The public use underlying the taking was unequivocally affirmed: "We do not sit to determine whether a particular housing project is or is not desirable. The concept of the public welfare is broad and inclusive. . . . The values it represents are spiritual as well as physical, aesthetic as well as monetary. It is within the power of the legislature to determine that the community should be beautiful as well as healthy, spacious as well as clean, well-balanced as well as carefully patrolled. In the present case, the Congress and its authorized agencies have made determinations that take into account a wide variety of values. It is not for us to reappraise them. If those who govern the District of Columbia decide that the Nation's Capital should be beautiful as well as sanitary, there is nothing in the Fifth Amendment that stands in the way."

In *Hawaii Housing Authority v. Midkiff*, the Court considered a Hawaii statute whereby fee title was taken from lessors and transferred to lessees (for just compensation) in order to reduce the concentration of land ownership. We unanimously upheld the statute and rejected the Ninth Circuit's view that it was "a naked attempt on the part of the state of Hawaii to take the property of A and transfer it to B solely for B's private use and benefit." Reaffirming *Berman*'s deferential approach to legislative judgments in this field, we concluded that the State's purpose of eliminating the "social and economic evils of a land oligopoly" qualified as a valid public use. Our opinion also rejected the contention that the mere fact that the State immediately transferred the properties to private individuals upon condemnation somehow diminished the public character of the taking. . . .

Those who govern the City were not confronted with the need to remove blight in the Fort Trumbull area, but their determination that the area was sufficiently distressed to justify a program of economic rejuvenation is entitled to our deference. The City has carefully formulated an economic development plan that it believes will provide appreciable benefits to the community, including—but by no means limited to—new jobs and increased tax revenue. As with other exercises in urban planning and development, the City is endeavoring to coordinate a variety of commercial, residential, and recreational uses of land, with the hope that they will form a whole greater than the sum of its parts. To effectuate this plan, the City has invoked a state statute that specifically authorizes the use of eminent domain to promote economic development. . . . Because that plan unquestionably serves a public purpose, the takings challenged here satisfy the public use requirement of the Fifth Amendment.

To avoid this result, petitioners urge us to adopt a new bright-line rule that economic development does not qualify as a public use. Putting aside the unpersuasive suggestion that the City's plan will provide only purely economic benefits, neither precedent nor logic supports petitioners' proposal. Promoting economic development is a traditional and long accepted function of government. There is, moreover, no principled way of distinguishing economic development from the other public purposes that we have recognized. . . .

Petitioners contend that using eminent domain for economic development impermissibly blurs the boundary between public and private takings. Again, our cases foreclose this objection. Quite simply, the government's pursuit of a public purpose will often benefit individual private parties. For example, in *Midkiff*, the forced transfer of property conferred a direct and significant benefit on those lessees who were previously unable to purchase their homes. . . .

It is further argued that without a bright-line rule nothing would stop a city from transferring citizen A's property to citizen B for the sole reason that citizen B will put the property to a more productive use and thus pay more taxes. Such a one-to-one transfer of property, executed outside the confines of an integrated development plan, is not presented in this case. While such an unusual exercise of government power would certainly raise a suspicion that a private purpose was afoot, the hypothetical cases posited by petitioners can be confronted if and when they arise. They do not warrant the crafting of an artificial restriction on the concept of public use.

Alternatively, petitioners maintain that for takings of this kind we should require a "reasonable certainty" that the expected public benefits will actually accrue. Such a rule, however, would represent an even greater departure from our precedent. "When the legislature's purpose is legitimate and its means are not irrational, our cases make clear that empirical debates over the wisdom of takings—no less than debates over the wisdom of other kinds of socioeconomic legislation—are not to be carried out in the federal courts." *Midkiff*. . . .

Just as we decline to second-guess the City's considered judgments about the efficacy of its development plan, we also decline to second-guess the

City's determinations as to what lands it needs to acquire in order to effectuate the project. "It is not for the courts to oversee the choice of the boundary line nor to sit in review on the size of a particular project area. Once the question of the public purpose has been decided, the amount and character of land to be taken for the project and the need for a particular tract to complete the integrated plan rests in the discretion of the legislative branch."

In affirming the City's authority to take petitioners' properties, we do not minimize the hardship that condemnations may entail, notwithstanding the payment of just compensation. We emphasize that nothing in our opinion precludes any State from placing further restrictions on its exercise of the takings power. Indeed, many States already impose "public use" requirements that are stricter than the federal baseline. Some of these requirements have been established as a matter of state constitutional law, while others are expressed in state eminent domain statutes that carefully limit the grounds upon which takings may be exercised. . . .

The judgment of the Supreme Court of Connecticut is affirmed.

□ *Justice KENNEDY, concurring.*

I join the opinion for the Court and add these further observations. This Court has declared that a taking should be upheld as consistent with the Public Use Clause, U.S. Const., Amdt. 5., as long as it is "rationally related to a conceivable public purpose." *Hawaii Housing Authority v. Midkiff*; see also *Berman v. Parker*, 348 U.S. 26 (1954). This deferential standard of review echoes the rational-basis test used to review economic regulation under the Due Process and Equal Protection Clauses. The determination that a rational-basis standard of review is appropriate does not, however, alter the fact that transfers intended to confer benefits on particular, favored private entities, and with only incidental or pretextual public benefits, are forbidden by the Public Use Clause.

A court applying rational-basis review under the Public Use Clause should strike down a taking that, by a clear showing, is intended to favor a particular private party, with only incidental or pretextual public benefits, just as a court applying rational-basis review under the Equal Protection Clause must strike down a government classification that is clearly intended to injure a particular class of private parties, with only incidental or pretextual public justifications. See *Cleburne v. Cleburne Living Center, Inc.*, 473 U.S. 432 (1985). As the trial court in this case was correct to observe, "Where the purpose [of a taking] is economic development and that development is to be carried out by private parties or private parties will be benefited, the court must decide if the stated public purpose—economic advantage to a city sorely in need of it—is only incidental to the benefits that will be confined on private parties of a development plan."

A court confronted with a plausible accusation of impermissible favoritism to private parties should treat the objection as a serious one and review the record to see if it has merit, though with the presumption that the government's actions were reasonable and intended to serve a public purpose. Here, the trial court conducted a careful and extensive inquiry into "whether, in fact, the development plan is of primary benefit to . . . the developer, and private businesses which may eventually locate in the plan area, and in that regard, only of incidental benefit to the city." The trial court considered testimony from government officials and corporate officers; documentary evidence of communications between these parties; respondents' awareness of

New London's depressed economic condition and evidence corroborating the validity of this concern; the substantial commitment of public funds by the State to the development project before most of the private beneficiaries were known; evidence that respondents reviewed a variety of development plans and chose a private developer from a group of applicants rather than picking out a particular transferee beforehand; and the fact that the other private beneficiaries of the project are still unknown because the office space proposed to be built has not yet been rented. The trial court concluded, based on these findings, that benefiting Pfizer was not "the primary motivation or effect of this development plan"; instead, "the primary motivation for [respondents] was to take advantage of Pfizer's presence." Likewise, the trial court concluded that "[t]here is nothing in the record to indicate that . . . [respondents] were motivated by a desire to aid [other] particular private entities." . . .

My agreement with the Court that a presumption of invalidity is not warranted for economic development takings in general, or for the particular takings at issue in this case, does not foreclose the possibility that a more stringent standard of review than that announced in *Berman* and *Midkiff* might be appropriate for a more narrowly drawn category of takings. There may be private transfers in which the risk of undetected impermissible favoritism of private parties is so acute that a presumption (rebuttable or otherwise) of invalidity is warranted under the Public Use Clause. This demanding level of scrutiny, however, is not required simply because the purpose of the taking is economic development.

This is not the occasion for conjecture as to what sort of cases might justify a more demanding standard, but it is appropriate to underscore aspects of the instant case that convince me no departure from *Berman* and *Midkiff* is appropriate here. This taking occurred in the context of a comprehensive development plan meant to address a serious city-wide depression, and the projected economic benefits of the project cannot be characterized as *de minimus*. The identity of most of the private beneficiaries were unknown at the time the city formulated its plans. The city complied with elaborate procedural requirements that facilitate review of the record and inquiry into the city's purposes. In sum, while there may be categories of cases in which the transfers are so suspicious, or the procedures employed so prone to abuse, or the purported benefits are so trivial or implausible, that courts should presume an impermissible private purpose, no such circumstances are present in this case.

□ *Justice O'CONNOR, with whom THE CHIEF JUSTICE, Justice SCALIA, and Justice THOMAS join, dissenting.*

Over two centuries ago, just after the Bill of Rights was ratified, Justice CHASE wrote: "An act of the Legislature (for I cannot call it a law) contrary to the great first principles of the social compact, cannot be considered a rightful exercise of legislative authority . . . . A few instances will suffice to explain what I mean . . . . [A] law that takes property from A. and gives it to B: It is against all reason and justice, for a people to entrust a Legislature with such powers; and, therefore, it cannot be presumed that they have done it." *Calder v. Bull*, 3 Dall. 386 (1798). Today the Court abandons this long-held, basic limitation on government power. Under the banner of economic development, all private property is now vulnerable to being taken and transferred to another private owner, so long as it might be upgraded—i.e., given to an owner who will use it in a way that the legislature deems more beneficial to the public—in the process. To reason, as the Court does, that the incidental public benefits resulting from the subsequent ordinary use of private property render economic development takings "for public use" is to wash out any distinction between private and public use of property—and thereby effectively to delete the words "for public use" from the Takings Clause of the Fifth Amendment. Accordingly I respectfully dissent. . . .

[W]e have read the Fifth Amendment's language to impose two distinct conditions on the exercise of eminent domain: "the taking must be for a 'public use' and 'just compensation' must be paid to the owner." *Brown v. Legal Foundation of Wash.*, 538 U.S. 216 (2003). These two limitations serve to protect "the security of Property," which Alexander Hamilton described to the Philadelphia Convention as one of the "great obj[ects] of Gov[ernment]." Together they ensure stable property ownership by providing safeguards against excessive, unpredictable, or unfair use of the government's eminent domain power—particularly against those owners who, for whatever reasons, may be unable to protect themselves in the political process against the majority's will.

While the Takings Clause presupposes that government can take private property without the owner's consent, the just compensation requirement spreads the cost of condemnations and thus "prevents the public from loading upon one individual more than his just share of the burdens of government." *Monongahela Nav. Co. v. United States*, 148 U.S. 312 (1893). The public use requirement, in turn, imposes a more basic limitation, circumscribing the very scope of the eminent domain power: Government may compel an individual to forfeit her property for the public's use, but not for the benefit of another private person. This requirement promotes fairness as well as security.

Where is the line between "public" and "private" property use? We give considerable deference to legislatures' determinations about what governmental activities will advantage the public. But were the political branches the sole arbiters of the public-private distinction, the Public Use Clause would amount to little more than hortatory fluff. An external, judicial check on how the public use requirement is interpreted, however limited, is necessary if this constraint on government power is to retain any meaning.

Our cases have generally identified three categories of takings that comply with the public use requirement, though it is in the nature of things that the boundaries between these categories are not always firm. Two are relatively straightforward and uncontroversial. First, the sovereign may transfer private property to public ownership—such as for a road, a hospital, or a military base. Second, the sovereign may transfer private property to private parties, often common carriers, who make the property available for the public's use—such as with a railroad, a public utility, or a stadium. But "public ownership" and "use-by-the-public" are sometimes too constricting and impractical ways to define the scope of the Public Use Clause. Thus we have allowed that, in certain circumstances and to meet certain exigencies, takings that serve a public purpose also satisfy the Constitution even if the property is destined for subsequent private use.

This case returns us for the first time in over 20 years to the hard question of when a purportedly "public purpose" taking meets the public use requirement. It presents an issue of first impression: Are economic development takings constitutional? I would hold that they are not. We are guided by two precedents about the taking of real property by eminent domain. In *Berman*, we upheld takings within a blighted neighborhood of Washington,

D.C. The neighborhood had so deteriorated that, for example, 64.3% of its dwellings were beyond repair. . . .

In *Midkiff*, we upheld a land condemnation scheme in Hawaii whereby title in real property was taken from lessors and transferred to lessees. At that time, the State and Federal Governments owned nearly 49% of the State's land, and another 47% was in the hands of only 72 private landowners. Concentration of land ownership was so dramatic that on the State's most urbanized island, Oahu, 22 landowners owned 72.5% of the fee simple titles. The Hawaii Legislature had concluded that the oligopoly in land ownership was "skewing the State's residential fee simple market, inflating land prices, and injuring the public tranquility and welfare," and therefore enacted a condemnation scheme for redistributing title.

In those decisions, we emphasized the importance of deferring to legislative judgments about public purpose. Because courts are ill-equipped to evaluate the efficacy of proposed legislative initiatives, we rejected as unworkable the idea of courts' "'deciding on what is and is not a governmental function and . . . invalidating legislation on the basis of their view on that question at the moment of decision, a practice which has proved impracticable in other fields.'" Likewise, we recognized our inability to evaluate whether, in a given case, eminent domain is a necessary means by which to pursue the legislature's ends.

Yet for all the emphasis on deference, *Berman* and *Midkiff* hewed to a bedrock principle without which our public use jurisprudence would collapse: "A purely private taking could not withstand the scrutiny of the public use requirement; it would serve no legitimate purpose of government and would thus be void." *Midkiff*. To protect that principle, those decisions reserved "a role for courts to play in reviewing a legislature's judgment of what constitutes a public use . . . [though] the Court in *Berman* made clear that it is 'an extremely narrow' one."

The Court's holdings in *Berman* and *Midkiff* were true to the principle underlying the Public Use Clause. In both those cases, the extraordinary, precondemnation use of the targeted property inflicted affirmative harm on society—in *Berman* through blight resulting from extreme poverty and in *Midkiff* through oligopoly resulting from extreme wealth. And in both cases, the relevant legislative body had found that eliminating the existing property use was necessary to remedy the harm. Thus a public purpose was realized when the harmful use was eliminated. Because each taking directly achieved a public benefit, it did not matter that the property was turned over to private use. Here, in contrast, New London does not claim that Susette Kelo's . . . well-maintained [home is] the source of any social harm. Indeed, it could not so claim without adopting the absurd argument that any single-family home that might be razed to make way for an apartment building, or any church that might be replaced with a retail store, or any small business that might be more lucrative if it were instead part of a national franchise, is inherently harmful to society and thus within the government's power to condemn.

In moving away from our decisions sanctioning the condemnation of harmful property use, the Court today significantly expands the meaning of public use. It holds that the sovereign may take private property currently put to ordinary private use, and give it over for new, ordinary private use, so long as the new use is predicted to generate some secondary benefit for the public—such as increased tax revenue, more jobs, maybe even aesthetic pleasure. But nearly any lawful use of real private property can be said to generate some incidental benefit to the public. Thus, if predicted (or even guaranteed) positive side-effects are enough to render transfer from one private party to another constitutional, then the words "for public use" do not realistically exclude any takings, and thus do not exert any constraint on the eminent domain power. . . .

It was possible after *Berman* and *Midkiff* to imagine unconstitutional transfers from A to B. Those decisions endorsed government intervention when private property use had veered to such an extreme that the public was suffering as a consequence. Today nearly all real property is susceptible to condemnation on the Court's theory. Any property may now be taken for the benefit of another private party, but the fallout from this decision will not be random. The beneficiaries are likely to be those citizens with disproportionate influence and power in the political process, including large corporations and development firms. As for the victims, the government now has license to transfer property from those with fewer resources to those with more. . . .

□ *Justice THOMAS, dissenting.*

Long ago, William Blackstone wrote that "the law of the land . . . postpone[s] even public necessity to the sacred and inviolable rights of private property." *Commentaries on the Laws of England* (1765). The Framers embodied that principle in the Constitution, allowing the government to take property not for "public necessity," but instead for "public use." Amdt. 5. Defying this understanding, the Court replaces the Public Use Clause with a "'[P]ublic [P]urpose'" Clause, a restriction that is satisfied, the Court instructs, so long as the purpose is "legitimate" and the means "not irrational." This deferential shift in phraseology enables the Court to hold, against all common sense, that a costly urban-renewal project whose stated purpose is a vague promise of new jobs and increased tax revenue, but which is also suspiciously agreeable to the Pfizer Corporation, is for a "public use."

I cannot agree. If such "economic development" takings are for a "public use," any taking is, and the Court has erased the Public Use Clause from our Constitution, as Justice O'CONNOR powerfully argues in dissent. I do not believe that this Court can eliminate liberties expressly enumerated in the Constitution and therefore join her dissenting opinion. Regrettably, however, the Court's error runs deeper than this. Today's decision is simply the latest in a string of our cases construing the Public Use Clause to be a virtual nullity, without the slightest nod to its original meaning. In my view, the Public Use Clause, originally understood, is a meaningful limit on the government's eminent domain power. Our cases have strayed from the Clause's original meaning, and I would reconsider them. . . .

The consequences of today's decision are not difficult to predict, and promise to be harmful. So-called "urban renewal" programs provide some compensation for the properties they take, but no compensation is possible for the subjective value of these lands to the individuals displaced and the indignity inflicted by uprooting them from their homes. Allowing the government to take property solely for public purposes is bad enough, but extending the concept of public purpose to encompass any economically beneficial goal guarantees that these losses will fall disproportionately on poor communities. Those communities are not only systematically less likely to put their lands to the highest and best social use, but are also the least politically powerful. If ever there were justification for intrusive judicial review of constitutional provisions that protect "discrete and insular minorities," *United States v. Carolene Products Co.*, 304 U.S. 144 (1938), surely that principle would apply with great force to the powerless groups and individuals the Public Use Clause protects. The deferential standard this Court has adopted for the Public Use Clause is therefore deeply perverse. It encourages "those citizens with disproportionate influence and power in the political process, including large corporations and development firms" to victimize the weak.

Those incentives have made the legacy of this Court's "public purpose" test an unhappy one. In the 1950's, no doubt emboldened in part by the expansive understanding of "public use" this Court adopted in *Berman*, cities "rushed to draw plans" for downtown development. "Of all the families displaced by urban renewal from 1949 through 1963, 63 percent of those whose race was known were nonwhite, and of these families, 56 percent of nonwhites and 38 percent of whites had incomes low enough to qualify for public housing, which, however, was seldom available to them." Public works projects in the 1950's and 1960's destroyed predominantly minority communities in St. Paul, Minnesota, and Baltimore, Maryland. In 1981, urban planners in Detroit, Michigan, uprooted the largely "lower-income and elderly" Poletown neighborhood for the benefit of the General Motors Corporation. Urban renewal projects have long been associated with the displacement of blacks; "[i]n cities across the country, urban renewal came to be known as 'Negro removal.'" Over 97 percent of the individuals forcibly removed from their homes by the "slum-clearance" project upheld by this Court in *Berman* were black. Regrettably, the predictable consequence of the Court's decision will be to exacerbate these effects. . . .

■ THE DEVELOPMENT OF LAW

Other Important Rulings on the Takings Clause

CASE	VOTE	RULING
Lingle v. Chevron, 125 S.Ct. 2074 (2005)	9:0	Writing for a unanimous Court, Justice O'Connor upheld Hawaii's law capping the rent paid by gasoline dealers and ruled that it was not an unconstitutional takings. The appellate court had applied a test, suggested in *Agins v. City of Tiburon*, 447 U.S. 255 (1980), that "[t]he application of a general zoning law to particular property effects a takings if the ordinance does not substantially advance state interests." But Justice O'Connor ruled that the "substantially advance state interests" test was *dictum* and inappropriate for determining when a takings of private property occurs. Instead, as other precedents established, in particular *Penn Central Transportation Co. v. New York*, 438 U.S. 104 (1978), a multi-factored and more deferential test should apply because taxes and fees, like that at issue here, are not per se takings.

Supreme Court Watch 2005

Volume Two

4

The Nationalization of the Bill of Rights

B | *The Rise and (Partial) Retreat of the "Due Process Revolution"*

In its 2002–2003 term the Court revisited the constitutionality of "Megan's Laws," which all fifty states have enacted and which require convicted sex offenders to register with state and local police, as well as to make available to the public their names, addresses, and photographs. These laws were enacted following the death of Megan Kanka, a New Jersey girl who was raped and murdered in 1994 by a sex offender in her neighborhood whose criminal history was unknown to her parents. Two convicted sex offenders challenged the constitutionality of Connecticut's law that, like those in nineteen other states, requires the public disclosure of personal information and DNA samples as well as the posting of the names, addresses, and photographs of convicted sex offenders on the Internet. A federal district court agreed that the publication and posting on the Web of offenders' personal information without first holding a hearing on their danger to society violated the guarantee of due process. The Court of Appeals for the Second Circuit agreed, but on appeal the Supreme Court reversed and found no due process violation because the registry requirement is based on a criminal conviction, not current dangerousness, in *Connecticut Department of Public Safety v. Doe*, 538 U.S. 1 (2003).

■ The Development of Law

Other Recent Rulings on Substantive and Procedural Due Process

CASE	VOTE	RULING
Deck v. Mississippi, 125 S.Ct. 2007 (2005)	7:2	Writing for the Court, Justice Breyer held that the shackling of a defendant during the sentencing phase of a capital trial is inherently prejudicial and runs afoul of the Fifth and Fourteenth Amendments, unless the use of visible shackles is justified by an "essential state interest." Justices Scalia and Thomas dissented.
Town of Castle Rock v. Gonzales, 125 S.Ct. 2796 (2005)	7:2	Writing for the Court, Justice Scalia ruled that Due Process Clauses do not protect everything deemed to be a government "benefit." Jessica Gonzales filed a suit for damages because the town's police failed to enforce a court-ordered restraining order against her estranged husband, who took her three children in violation of the order and murdered them. Under Colorado law, police are required to enforce restraining orders and thus Gonzales argued that that was an entitlement and government benefit. In rejecting that claim, Justice Scalia observed: "The procedural component of the Due Process Clause does not protect everything that might be described as a 'benefit,'" and reaffirmed the holding in *Board of Regents of State Colleges v. Roth,* 408 U.S. (1972) that "To have a property interest in a benefit, a person clearly must have more than an abstract need or desire" and "more than a unilateral expectation of it. He must, instead, have a legitimate claim of entitlement to it." Justice Souter concurred and Justices Stevens and Ginsburg dissented.

5

Freedom of Expression and Association

Rumsfeld v. Forum for Academic and Institutional Rights

(No. 04-1152) (reprise; discussed in Vol. 1, Chapter 3)

D | *Commercial Speech*

■ The Development of Law

Other Recent Rulings on Commercial Speech and the First Amendment

CASE	VOTE	RULING
Johanns v. Livestock Marketing Association, 125 S.Ct. 2055 (2005)	6:3	Writing for the Court, Justice Scalia upheld the beef promotion and Research Act of 1985, which requires cattle producers to pay $1 for each head of cattle in order to finance a marketing campaign, "Beef: It's What's for Dinner." Although the Court invalidated a similar program for the marketing of mushrooms, in *United States v. United Foods*, 533 U.S. 405

(2001), it did not address the question of whether such programs are "government speech." Some independent cattle producers objected to the program, contending that it constituted unconstitutionally "compelled speech." Justice Scalia, however, ruled that "government speech" is not subject to ordinary First Amendment analysis. In his words: "Compelled funding of government speech does not alone raise First Amendment concerns. . . . Citizens may challenge compelled support of private speech, but have no First Amendment right not to fund government speech." Justices Stevens, Kennedy, and Souter dissented.

6

FREEDOM FROM AND OF RELIGION

A | *The (Dis)Establishment Clause*

In a continuation of a dialogue between Congress and the Court over congressional power, religious freedom, and the tensions between the First Amendment's (Dis)Establishment and Free Exercise clauses, the Court handed down *Cutter v. Wilkinson* (excerpted below), upholding the Religious Land Use and Institutionalized Persons Act (RLUIPA) of 2000.

In two other widely watched cases, the Court also revisited the controversy over the public display of the Ten Commandments and other religious symbols, addressed in *Stone v. Graham*, 449 U.S. 39 (1980), which held unconstitutional a Kentucky statute requiring the posting of the Ten Commandments in every public school room; and in *County of Allegheny v. American Civil Liberties Union, Greater Pittsburgh Chapter*, 492 U.S. 573 (1989) (see the "constitutional history" box in Vol. 2, Ch. 6). In both cases, the Court split five to four. In *Van Orden v. Perry* (excerpted below), writing for a plurality Chief Justice Rehnquist held that the erection of a six-foot granite monument on which the Ten Commandments were chiseled did not violate the First Amendment (Dis)Establishment Clause. Justices Stevens, O'Connor, Souter, and Ginsburg dissented. However, in *McCreary v. American Civil Liberties Union of Kentucky* (excerpted below), Justice Souter ruled that two Kentucky counties violated the First Amendment by prominently displaying the Ten Commandments in their courthouses. Chief Rehnquist and Justices Scalia, Kennedy, and Thomas dissented. In both cases, Justice Breyer cast the pivotal vote and formed bare majorities. He did so on pragmatic grounds, reasoning that the Texas monument had stood unchallenged for over 40 years, whereas the Kentucky displays immediately sparked controversy and appeared to clearly aim at endorsing religion. The rulings are certain to invite some confusion and further litigation. As the Court is currently constituted, a bare majority appears willing to uphold the display of religious symbols, surrounded by other symbols or monuments, but to rule against more recently installed public displays of religious symbols if they have solely a religious purpose.

Cutter v. Wilkinson

125 S.Ct. 2113 (2005)

In response to the invalidation of the Religious Freedom Restoration Act (RFRA) of 1993 in *City of Boerne v. Flores*, 521 U.S. 507 (1997) (excerpted in Vol. 2, Ch. 6), Congress enacted the Religious Land Use and Institutionalized Persons Act (RLUIPA) of 2000. The RFRA had aimed to reestablish the test for determining religious freedom under the Free Exercise clause that was discarded in *Employment Division, Department of Human Resources of Oregon v. Smith*, 494 U.S. 872 (1990) (excerpted in Vol. 2, Ch. 6). But *City of Boerne* held that Congress lacked the authority to enact the law under its power in Section 5 of the Fourteenth Amendment, because that power is only remedial and may not be relied on to define the scope of constitutional rights. In turn, Congress passed the narrower RLUIPA based on its powers under the Spending and Commerce clauses. The RLUIPA specifies that state and local governments that receive federal funding for services may not "impose a substantial burden on the religious exercise of a person residing in or confined to an institution," unless the burden is necessary to achieving a "compelling" governmental purpose.

When inmates in Ohio prisons were denied special services for their observance of rituals associated with Wicca, Satanism, Asatru, and the Church of Jesus Christ Christian, a clinical legal program at the Ohio State University Moritz College of Law took up their representation and sued the state for violating the RLUIPA. The state countered that the RLUIPA violated the (Dis)Establishment clause, would compromise prison security, and prove costly. A federal district court refused to dismiss the suit, but the Court of Appeals for the Sixth Circuit ruled that the RLUIPA violated the (Dis)Establishment clause "by giving greater protection to religious rights than to other constitutionally protected rights." That decision was appealed and the Court granted review.

The appellate court's decision was reversed by a unanimous Court. Justice Ginsburg delivered the opinion of the Court and Justice Thomas filed a concurring opinion.

□ *Justice GINSBURG delivered the opinion of the Court.*

Section 3 of the Religious Land Use and Institutionalized Persons Act of 2000 (RLUIPA) provides in part: "No government shall impose a substantial burden on the religious exercise of a person residing in or confined to an institution," unless the burden furthers "a compelling governmental interest," and does so by "the least restrictive means." . . .

"This Court has long recognized that the government may . . . accommodate religious practices . . . without violating the Establishment Clause." *Hobbie v. Unemployment Appeals Comm'n of Fla.*, 480 U.S. 136 (1987). Just last Term, in *Locke v. Davey*, 540 U.S. 712 (2004), the Court reaffirmed that "there is room for play in the joints between" the Free Exercise and Establishment Clauses, allowing the government to accommodate religion beyond free exercise requirements, without offense to the Establishment Clause. But Section 3 of RLUIPA, we hold, does not, on its face, exceed the limits of permissible government accommodation of religious practices.

RLUIPA is the latest of long-running congressional efforts to accord religious exercise heightened protection from government-imposed burdens, consistent with this Court's precedents. Ten years before RLUIPA's enactment, the Court held, in *Employment Div., Dept. of Human Resources of Ore. v. Smith*, 494 U.S. 872 (1990), that the First Amendment's Free Exercise Clause does not inhibit enforcement of otherwise valid laws of general application that incidentally burden religious conduct. In particular, we ruled that the Free Exercise Clause did not bar Oregon from enforcing its blanket ban on peyote possession with no allowance for sacramental use of the drug. Accordingly, the State could deny unemployment benefits to persons dismissed from their jobs because of their religiously inspired peyote use. The Court recognized, however, that the political branches could shield religious exercise through legislative accommodation, for example, by making an exception to proscriptive drug laws for sacramental peyote use.

Responding to *Smith*, Congress enacted the Religious Freedom Restoration Act of 1993 (RFRA). RFRA "prohibits '[g]overnment' from 'substantially burden[ing]' a person's exercise of religion even if the burden results from a rule of general applicability unless the government can demonstrate the burden '(1) is in furtherance of a compelling governmental interest; and (2) is the least restrictive means of furthering that compelling governmental interest.'" *City of Boerne v. Flores*, 521 U.S. 507 (1997). "[U]niversal" in its coverage, RFRA "applie[d] to all Federal and State law," but notably lacked a Commerce Clause underpinning or a Spending Clause limitation to recipients of federal funds. In *City of Boerne*, this Court invalidated RFRA as applied to States and their subdivisions, holding that the Act exceeded Congress's remedial powers under the Fourteenth Amendment.

Congress again responded, this time by enacting RLUIPA. Less sweeping than RFRA, and invoking federal authority under the Spending and Commerce Clauses, RLUIPA targets two areas: Section 2 of the Act concerns land-use regulation; Section 3 relates to religious exercise by institutionalized persons. Section 3, at issue here, provides that "[n]o [state or local] government shall impose a substantial burden on the religious exercise of a person residing in or confined to an institution," unless the government shows that the burden furthers "a compelling governmental interest" and does so by "the least restrictive means." The Act defines "religious exercise" to include "any exercise of religion, whether or not compelled by, or central to, a system of religious belief." Section 3 applies when "the substantial burden [on religious exercise] is imposed in a program or activity that receives Federal financial assistance," or "the substantial burden affects, or removal of that substantial burden would affect, commerce with foreign nations, among the several States, or with Indian tribes."

The Religion Clauses of the First Amendment provide: "Congress shall make no law respecting an establishment of religion, or prohibiting the free exercise thereof." The first of the two Clauses, commonly called the Establishment Clause, commands a separation of church and state. The second, the Free Exercise Clause, requires government respect for, and noninterference with, the religious beliefs and practices of our Nation's people. While the two Clauses express complementary values, they often exert conflicting pressures.

Our decisions recognize that "there is room for play in the joints" between the Clauses, some space for legislative action neither compelled by the Free Exercise Clause nor prohibited by the Establishment Clause. In accord with the majority of Courts of Appeals that have ruled on the question, we hold that Section 3 of RLUIPA fits within the corridor between the Relgion Clauses: On its face, the Act qualifies as a permissible legislative accommodation of religion that is not barred by the Establishment Clause.

Foremost, we find RLUIPA's institutionalized-persons provision compatible with the Establishment Clause because it alleviates exceptional government-created burdens on private religious exercise. Furthermore, the Act on its face does not founder on shoals our prior decisions have identified: Properly applying RLUIPA, courts must take adequate account of the burdens a requested accommodation may impose on nonbeneficiaries; and they must be satisfied that the Act's prescriptions are and will be administered neutrally among different faiths. . . .

RLUIPA thus protects institutionalized persons who are unable freely to attend to their religious needs and are therefore dependent on the government's permission and accommodation for exercise of their religion. . . . We do not read RLUIPA to elevate accommodation of religious observances over an institution's need to maintain order and safety. Our decisions indicate that an accommodation must be measured so that it does not override other significant interests.

We have no cause to believe that RLUIPA would not be applied in an appropriately balanced way, with particular sensitivity to security concerns. While the Act adopts a "compelling governmental interest" standard, "[c]ontext matters" in the application of that standard. Lawmakers supporting RLUIPA were mindful of the urgency of discipline, order, safety, and security in penal institutions. . . .

For the reasons stated, the judgment of the United States Court of Appeals for the Sixth Circuit is reversed, and the case is remanded for further proceedings consistent with this opinion.

□ *Justice THOMAS, concurring.*

I write to explain why a proper historical understanding of the Clause as a federalism provision leads to the same conclusion.

The Establishment Clause provides that "Congress shall make no law respecting an establishment of religion." As I have explained, an important function of the Clause was to "ma[ke] clear that Congress could not interfere with state establishments." *Elk Grove Unified School Dist. v. Newdow*, 542 U.S. 1 (2004) (opinion concurring in judgment). The Clause, then, "is best understood as a federalism provision" that "protects state establishments from federal interference." Ohio contends that this federalism understanding of the Clause prevents federal oversight of state choices within the "'play in the joints'" between the Free Exercise and Establishment Clauses. *Locke v. Davey*, 540 U.S. 712 (2004). In other words, Ohio asserts that the Clause protects the States from federal interference with otherwise constitutionally permissible choices regarding religious policy. In Ohio's view, RLUIPA intrudes on such state policy choices and hence violates the Clause.

Ohio's vision of the range of protected state authority overreads the Clause. . . . To proscribe Congress from making laws "respecting an establishment of religion" . . . was to forbid legislation respecting coercive state establishments, not to preclude Congress from legislating on religion generally. . . .

In short, the view that the Establishment Clause precludes Congress from legislating respecting religion lacks historical provenance, at least based on the history of which I am aware. Even when enacting laws that bind the States pursuant to valid exercises of its enumerated powers, Congress need not observe strict separation between church and state, or steer clear of the subject of religion. It need only refrain from making laws "respecting an establishment of religion"; it must not interfere with a state establishment of religion. For example, Congress presumably could not require a State to establish a religion any more than it could preclude a State from establishing a religion.

On its face—the relevant inquiry, as this is a facial challenge—RLUIPA is not a law "respecting an establishment of religion." RLUIPA provides, as relevant: "No government shall impose a substantial burden on the religious exercise of a person residing in or confined to an institution, . . . even if the burden results from a rule of general applicability, unless the government demonstrates that imposition of the burden on that person," first, "further[s] a compelling governmental interest," and second, "is the least restrictive means of furthering that compelling governmental interest." This provision does not prohibit or interfere with state establishments, since no State has established (or constitutionally could establish, given an incorporated Clause) a religion. Nor does the provision require a State to establish a religion: It does not force a State to coerce religious observance or payment of taxes supporting clergy, or require a State to prefer one religious sect over another. It is a law respecting religion, but not one respecting an establishment of religion. . . .

It also bears noting that Congress, pursuant to its Spending Clause authority, conditioned the States' receipt of federal funds on their compliance with RLUIPA. RLUIPA may well exceed the spending power. Nonetheless, while Congress's condition stands, the States subject themselves to that condition by voluntarily accepting federal funds. The States' voluntary acceptance of Congress's condition undercuts Ohio's argument that Congress is encroaching on its turf.

Van Orden v. Perry

125 S.Ct. 2854 (2005)

In the 1950s and 1960s, the Fraternal Order of Eagles, a national civic organization, erected hundreds of granite Ten Commandments monuments around the country. One of these was among 21 historical markers and 17 monuments in a 22-acre public park surrounding the Texas State Capitol in Austin. The Ten Commandments are inscribed on a six-foot high monolith which the Eagles erected and donated to the city in an effort to combat juvenile delinquency. Thomas Van Orden, a lawyer who is homeless and who frequently visits the Capitol, where he spends his days in the law library of the state supreme court building, filed a lawsuit in 2001, contending that the monument violated the First Amendment (Dis)Establishment Clause. A federal district court held that, amid the other monuments, the display of the Ten Commandments had a secular purpose. That decision was affirmed by the Court of Appeals for the Fifth Circuit, and Van Orden appealed.

The appellate court's decision was affirmed by a five to four vote. Chief Justice Rehnquist delivered a plurality opinion for the Court, which Justices Scalia, Kennedy, and Thomas joined. Justices Scalia, Thomas, and Breyer each filed concurring opinions. Justices Stevens, O'Connor, Souter, and Ginsburg dissented.

□ *THE CHIEF JUSTICE announced the judgment of the Court and delivered an opinion, in which Justice SCALIA, Justice KENNEDY, and Justice THOMAS join.*

Our cases, Januslike, point in two directions in applying the Establishment Clause. One face looks toward the strong role played by religion and religious traditions throughout our Nation's history. As we observed in *School Dist. of Abington Township v. Schempp*, 374 U.S. 203 (1963): "It is true that religion has been closely identified with our history and government . . . The fact that the Founding Fathers believed devotedly that there was a God and that the unalienable rights of man were rooted in Him is clearly evidenced in their writings, from the Mayflower Compact to the Constitution itself. . . . It can be truly said, therefore, that today, as in the beginning, our national life reflects a religious people who, in the words of Madison, are 'earnestly praying, as . . . in duty bound, that the Supreme Lawgiver of the Universe . . . guide them into every measure which may be worthy of his [blessing. . . .]'" The other face looks toward the principle that governmental intervention in religious matters can itself endanger religious freedom.

This case, like all Establishment Clause challenges, presents us with the difficulty of respecting both faces. Our institutions presuppose a Supreme Being, yet these institutions must not press religious observances upon their citizens. One face looks to the past in acknowledgment of our Nation's heritage, while the other looks to the present in demanding a separation between church and state. Reconciling these two faces requires that we neither abdicate our responsibility to maintain a division between church and state nor evince a hostility to religion by disabling the government from in some ways recognizing our religious heritage. . . .

These two faces are evident in representative cases both upholding and invalidating laws under the Establishment Clause. Over the last 25 years, we have sometimes pointed to *Lemon v. Kurtzman*, 403 U.S. 602 (1971), as providing the governing test in Establishment Clause challenges. Compare *Wallace v. Jaffree*, 472 U.S. 38 (1985) (applying *Lemon*), with *Marsh v. Chambers*, 463

U.S. 783 (1983) (not applying *Lemon*). Yet, just two years after *Lemon* was decided, we noted that the factors identified in *Lemon* serve as "no more than helpful signposts." *Hunt v. McNair*, 413 U.S. 734 (1973). Many of our recent cases simply have not applied the *Lemon* test. See, e.g., *Zelman v. Simmons-Harris*, 536 U.S. 639 (2002); *Good News Club v. Milford Central School*, 533 U.S. 98 (2001). Others have applied it only after concluding that the challenged practice was invalid under a different Establishment Clause test.

Whatever may be the fate of the *Lemon* test in the larger scheme of Establishment Clause jurisprudence, we think it not useful in dealing with the sort of passive monument that Texas has erected on its Capitol grounds. Instead, our analysis is driven both by the nature of the monument and by our Nation's history. As we explained in *Lynch v. Donnelly*, 465 U.S. 668 (1984): "There is an unbroken history of official acknowledgment by all three branches of government of the role of religion in American life from at least 1789." For example, both Houses passed resolutions in 1789 asking President George Washington to issue a Thanksgiving Day Proclamation to "recommend to the people of the United States a day of public thanksgiving and prayer, to be observed by acknowledging, with grateful hearts, the many and signal favors of Almighty God." President Washington's proclamation directly attributed to the Supreme Being the foundations and successes of our young Nation. . . .

Recognition of the role of God in our Nation's heritage has also been reflected in our decisions. We have acknowledged, for example, that "religion has been closely identified with our history and government," *School Dist. of Abington Township v. Schempp*, and that "[t]he history of man is inseparable from the history of religion," *Engel v. Vitale*, 370 U.S. 421 (1962). This recognition has led us to hold that the Establishment Clause permits a state legislature to open its daily sessions with a prayer by a chaplain paid by the State. *Marsh v. Chambers*. Such a practice, we thought, was "deeply embedded in the history and tradition of this country." With similar reasoning, we have upheld laws, which originated from one of the Ten Commandments, that prohibited the sale of merchandise on Sunday. *McGowan v. Maryland*, 366 U.S. 420 (1961).

In this case we are faced with a display of the Ten Commandments on government property outside the Texas State Capitol. Such acknowledgments of the role played by the Ten Commandments in our Nation's heritage are common throughout America. We need only look within our own Courtroom. Since 1935, Moses has stood, holding two tablets that reveal portions of the Ten Commandments written in Hebrew, among other lawgivers in the south frieze. Representations of the Ten Commandments adorn the metal gates lining the north and south sides of the Courtroom as well as the doors leading into the Courtroom. Moses also sits on the exterior east facade of the building holding the Ten Commandments tablets. . . .

Our opinions, like our building, have recognized the role the Decalogue plays in America's heritage. The Executive and Legislative Branches have also acknowledged the historical role of the Ten Commandments. These displays and recognitions of the Ten Commandments bespeak the rich American tradition of religious acknowledgments.

Of course, the Ten Commandments are religious—they were so viewed at their inception and so remain. The monument, therefore, has religious significance. According to Judeo-Christian belief, the Ten Commandments were given to Moses by God on Mt. Sinai. But Moses was a lawgiver as well as a religious leader. And the Ten Commandments have an undeniable historical meaning, as the foregoing examples demonstrate. Simply having religious content or promoting a message consistent with a religious doctrine does not run afoul of the Establishment Clause.

There are, of course, limits to the display of religious messages or symbols. For example, we held unconstitutional a Kentucky statute requiring the posting of the Ten Commandments in every public schoolroom. *Stone v. Graham*, 449 U.S. 39 (1980). In the classroom context, we found that the Kentucky statute had an improper and plainly religious purpose. As evidenced by *Stone's* almost exclusive reliance upon two of our school prayer cases (citing *School Dist. of Abington Township v. Schempp*, 374 U.S. 203 (1963), and *Engel v. Vitale*, 370 U.S. 421 (1962)), it stands as an example of the fact that we have "been particularly vigilant in monitoring compliance with the Establishment Clause in elementary and secondary schools," *Edwards v. Aguillard*, 482 U.S. 578 (1987). Indeed, *Edwards v. Aguillard* recognized that *Stone*—along with *Schempp* and *Engel*—was a consequence of the "particular concerns that arise in the context of public elementary and secondary schools." Neither *Stone* itself nor subsequent opinions have indicated that *Stone's* holding would extend to a legislative chamber or to capitol grounds.

The placement of the Ten Commandments monument on the Texas State Capitol grounds is a far more passive use of those texts than was the case in *Stone*, where the text confronted elementary school students every day. Indeed, Van Orden, the petitioner here, apparently walked by the monument for a number of years before bringing this lawsuit. The monument is therefore also quite different from the prayers involved in *Schempp* and *Lee v. Weisman* [505 U.S. 577 (1992)]. Texas has treated her Capitol grounds monuments as representing the several strands in the State's political and legal history. The inclusion of the Ten Commandments monument in this group has a dual significance, partaking of both religion and government. We cannot say that Texas's display of this monument violates the Establishment Clause of the First Amendment.

□ *Justice BREYER, concurring in the judgment.*

In *School Dist. of Abington Township v. Schempp*, 374 U.S. 203 (1963), Justice GOLDBERG, joined by Justice HARLAN, wrote, in respect to the First Amendment's Religion Clauses, that there is "no simple and clear measure which by precise application can readily and invariably demark the permissible from the impermissible." One must refer instead to the basic purposes of those Clauses. They seek to "assure the fullest possible scope of religious liberty and tolerance for all." They seek to avoid that divisiveness based upon religion that promotes social conflict, sapping the strength of government and religion alike. They seek to maintain that "separation of church and state" that has long been critical to the "peaceful dominion that religion exercises in [this] country," where the "spirit of religion" and the "spirit of freedom" are productively "united," "reign[ing] together" but in separate spheres "on the same soil." A. de Tocqueville, *Democracy in America* (1835). They seek to further the basic principles set forth today by Justice *O'CONNOR* in her concurring opinion in *McCreary County v. American Civil Liberties Union of Ky.*

The Court has made clear, as Justices GOLDBERG and HARLAN noted, that the realization of these goals means that government must "neither engage in nor compel religious practices," that it must "effect no favoritism among sects or between religion and nonreligion," and that it must "work deterrence of no religious belief." The government must avoid excessive interference with, or promotion of, religion. But the Establishment Clause does not compel the government to purge from the public sphere all that in any way partakes of the religious. Such absolutism is not only inconsistent with our national traditions, but would also tend to promote the kind of social conflict the Establishment Clause seeks to avoid.

Thus, as Justices GOLDBERG and HARLAN pointed out, the Court has found no single mechanical formula that can accurately draw the constitutional line in every case. Where the Establishment Clause is at issue, tests designed to measure "neutrality" alone are insufficient, both because it is sometimes difficult to determine when a legal rule is "neutral," and because "untutored devotion to the concept of neutrality can lead to invocation or approval of results which partake not simply of that noninterference and noninvolvement with the religious which the Constitution commands, but of a brooding and pervasive devotion to the secular and a passive, or even active, hostility to the religious."

Neither can this Court's other tests readily explain the Establishment Clause's tolerance, for example, of the prayers that open legislative meetings; certain references to, and invocations of, the Deity in the public words of public officials; the public references to God on coins, decrees, and buildings; or the attention paid to the religious objectives of certain holidays, including Thanksgiving.

If the relation between government and religion is one of separation, but not of mutual hostility and suspicion, one will inevitably find difficult borderline cases. And in such cases, I see no test-related substitute for the exercise of legal judgment. That judgment is not a personal judgment. Rather, as in all constitutional cases, it must reflect and remain faithful to the underlying purposes of the Clauses, and it must take account of context and consequences measured in light of those purposes. While the Court's prior tests provide useful guideposts—and might well lead to the same result the Court reaches today—no exact formula can dictate a resolution to such fact-intensive cases.

The case before us is a borderline case. It concerns a large granite monument bearing the text of the Ten Commandments located on the grounds of the Texas State Capitol. On the one hand, the Commandments' text undeniably has a religious message, invoking, indeed emphasizing, the Deity. On the other hand, focusing on the text of the Commandments alone cannot conclusively resolve this case. Rather, to determine the message that the text here conveys, we must examine how the text is used. And that inquiry requires us to consider the context of the display.

In certain contexts, a display of the tablets of the Ten Commandments can convey not simply a religious message but also a secular moral message (about proper standards of social conduct). And in certain contexts, a display of the tablets can also convey a historical message (about a historic relation between those standards and the law)—a fact that helps to explain the display of those tablets in dozens of courthouses throughout the Nation, including the Supreme Court of the United States.

Here the tablets have been used as part of a display that communicates not simply a religious message, but a secular message as well. The circumstances surrounding the display's placement on the capitol grounds and its physical setting suggest that the State itself intended the latter, nonreligious aspects of the tablets' message to predominate. And the monument's 40-year history on the Texas state grounds indicates that that has been its effect.

The group that donated the monument, the Fraternal Order of Eagles, a private civic (and primarily secular) organization, while interested in the religious aspect of the Ten Commandments, sought to highlight the Commandments' role in shaping civic morality as part of that organization's efforts to combat juvenile delinquency. The Eagles' consultation with a committee composed of members of several faiths in order to find a nonsectarian text underscores the group's ethics-based motives. The tablets, as displayed on the monument, prominently acknowledge that the Eagles donated the display, a factor which, though not sufficient, thereby further distances the State itself from the religious aspect of the Commandments' message.

The physical setting of the monument, moreover, suggests little or nothing of the sacred. The monument sits in a large park containing 17 monuments and 21 historical markers, all designed to illustrate the "ideals" of those who settled in Texas and of those who have lived there since that time. . . .

If these factors provide a strong, but not conclusive, indication that the Commandments' text on this monument conveys a predominantly secular message, a further factor is determinative here. As far as I can tell, 40 years passed in which the presence of this monument, legally speaking, went unchallenged (until the single legal objection raised by petitioner). And I am not aware of any evidence suggesting that this was due to a climate of intimidation. Hence, those 40 years suggest more strongly than can any set of formulaic tests that few individuals, whatever their system of beliefs, are likely to have understood the monument as amounting, in any significantly detrimental way, to a government effort to favor a particular religious sect, primarily to promote religion over nonreligion, to "engage in" any "religious practic[e]," to "compel" any "religious practic[e]," or to "work deterrence" of any "religious belief." *Schempp* (GOLDBERG, J., concurring). Those 40 years suggest that the public visiting the capitol grounds has considered the religious aspect of the tablets' message as part of what is a broader moral and historical message reflective of a cultural heritage.

This case, moreover, is distinguishable from instances where the Court has found Ten Commandments displays impermissible. The display is not on the grounds of a public school, where, given the impressionability of the young, government must exercise particular care in separating church and state. This case also differs from *McCreary County*, where the short (and stormy) history of the courthouse Commandments' displays demonstrates the substantially religious objectives of those who mounted them, and the effect of this readily apparent objective upon those who view them. . . .

For these reasons, I believe that the Texas display—serving a mixed but primarily nonreligious purpose, not primarily "advanc[ing]" or "inhibit[ing] religion," and not creating an "excessive government entanglement with religion,"—might satisfy this Court's more formal Establishment Clause tests. *Lemon*. But, as I have said, in reaching the conclusion that the Texas display falls on the permissible side of the constitutional line, I rely less upon a literal application of any particular test than upon consideration of the basic purposes of the First Amendment's Religion Clauses themselves. This display has stood apparently uncontested for nearly two generations. That experience helps us understand that as a practical matter of degree this display is unlikely to prove divisive. And this matter of degree is, I believe, critical in a borderline case such as this one.

At the same time, to reach a contrary conclusion here based primarily upon the religious nature of the tablets' text would, I fear, lead the law to exhibit a hostility toward religion that has no place in our Establishment Clause traditions. Such a holding might well encourage disputes concerning the removal of longstanding depictions of the Ten Commandments from public buildings across the Nation. And it could thereby create the very kind of religiously based divisiveness that the Establishment Clause seeks to avoid.

In light of these considerations, I cannot agree with today's plurality's analysis. Nor can I agree with Justice SCALIA's dissent in *McCreary County*. I do agree with Justice O'CONNOR's statement of principles in *McCreary County*, though I disagree with her evaluation of the evidence as it bears on the application of those principles to this case.

□ *Justice SCALIA, concurring.*

I join the opinion of THE CHIEF JUSTICE because I think it accurately reflects our current Establishment Clause jurisprudence—or at least the Establishment Clause jurisprudence we currently apply some of the time. I would prefer to reach the same result by adopting an Establishment Clause jurisprudence that is in accord with our Nation's past and present practices, and that can be consistently applied—the central relevant feature of which is that there is nothing unconstitutional in a State's favoring religion generally, honoring God through public prayer and acknowledgment, or, in a nonproselytizing manner, venerating the Ten Commandments.

□ *Justice THOMAS, concurring.*

The Court holds that the Ten Commandments monument found on the Texas State Capitol grounds does not violate the Establishment Clause. Rather than trying to suggest meaninglessness where there is meaning, THE CHIEF JUSTICE rightly recognizes that the monument has "religious significance." He properly recognizes the role of religion in this Nation's history and the permissibility of government displays acknowledging that history. For those reasons, I join THE CHIEF JUSTICE's opinion in full.

This case would be easy if the Court were willing to abandon the inconsistent guideposts it has adopted for addressing Establishment Clause challenges, and return to the original meaning of the Clause. I have previously suggested that the Clause's text and history "resis[t] incorporation" against the States. See *Elk Grove Unified School Dist. v. Newdow*, 542 U.S. 1 (2004). If the Establishment Clause does not restrain the States, then it has no application here, where only state action is at issue.

Even if the Clause is incorporated, or if the Free Exercise Clause limits the power of States to establish religions, our task would be far simpler if we returned to the original meaning of the word "establishment" than it is under the various approaches this Court now uses. The Framers understood an establishment "necessarily [to] involve actual legal coercion." *Newdow* (THOMAS, J., concurring in judgment); *Lee v. Weisman*, 505 U.S. 577 (1992) (SCALIA, J., dissenting) ("The coercion that was a hallmark of historical establishments of religion was coercion of religious orthodoxy and of financial support by force of law and threat of penalty"). "In other words, establishment at the founding involved, for example, mandatory observance or mandatory payment of taxes supporting ministers." And "government practices that have nothing to do with creating or maintaining ... coercive state establishments" simply do not "implicate the possible liberty interest of being free from coercive state establishments." *Newdow* (THOMAS, J., concurring in judgment).

There is no question that, based on the original meaning of the Establishment Clause, the Ten Commandments display at issue here is constitutional. In no sense does Texas compel petitioner Van Orden to do anything. The only injury to him is that he takes offense at seeing the monument as he passes it on his way to the Texas Supreme Court Library. He need not stop to read it or even to look at it, let alone to express support for it or adopt the Commandments as guides for his life. The mere presence of the monument along his path involves no coercion and thus does not violate the Establishment Clause.

Returning to the original meaning would do more than simplify our task. It also would avoid the pitfalls present in the Court's current approach to such challenges. This Court's precedent elevates the trivial to the proverbial "federal case," by making benign signs and postings subject to challenge. Yet even as it does so, the Court's precedent attempts to avoid declaring all religious symbols and words of longstanding tradition unconstitutional, by counterfactually declaring them of little religious significance. Even when the Court's cases recognize that such symbols have religious meaning, they adopt an unhappy compromise that fails fully to account for either the adherent's or the nonadherent's beliefs, and provides no principled way to choose between them. Even worse, the incoherence of the Court's decisions in this area renders the Establishment Clause impenetrable and incapable of consistent application. All told, this Court's jurisprudence leaves courts, governments, and believers and nonbelievers alike confused—an observation that is hardly new. . . .

While the Court correctly rejects the challenge to the Ten Commandments monument on the Texas Capitol grounds, a more fundamental rethinking of our Establishment Clause jurisprudence remains in order.

□ *Justice SOUTER, with whom Justice STEVENS and Justice GINSBURG join, dissenting.*

Although the First Amendment's Religion Clauses have not been read to mandate absolute governmental neutrality toward religion, cf. *Sherbert v. Verner*, 374 U.S. 398 (1963), the Establishment Clause requires neutrality as a general rule, e.g., *Everson v. Board of Ed. of Ewing*, 330 U.S. 1 (1947), and thus expresses Madison's condemnation of "employ[ing] Religion as an engine of Civil policy," *Memorial and Remonstrance Against Religious Assessments*. A governmental display of an obviously religious text cannot be squared with neutrality, except in a setting that plausibly indicates that the statement is not placed in view with a predominant purpose on the part of government either to adopt the religious message or to urge its acceptance by others.

Until today, only one of our cases addressed the constitutionality of posting the Ten Commandments, *Stone v. Graham*, 449 U.S. 39 (1980). A Kentucky statute required posting the Commandments on the walls of public school classrooms, and the Court described the State's purpose (relevant under the tripartite test laid out in *Lemon v. Kurtzman*, 403 U.S. 602 (1971)) as being at odds with the obligation of religious neutrality. [T]he simple realities [are] that the Ten Commandments constitute a religious statement, that their message is inherently religious, and that the purpose of singling them out in a display is clearly the same.

Thus, a pedestrian happening upon the monument at issue here needs no training in religious doctrine to realize that the statement of the Commandments, quoting God himself, proclaims that the will of the divine being is the source of obligation to obey the rules, including the facially secular ones. In this case, moreover, the text is presented to give particular prominence to the Commandments' first sectarian reference, "I am the Lord thy God." That proclamation is centered on the stone and written in slightly larger letters than the subsequent recitation. To ensure that the religious nature of the monument is clear to even the most casual passerby, the word "Lord" appears in all capital letters (as does the word "am"), so that the most eye-catching segment of the quotation is the declaration "I AM the LORD thy God." What follows, of course, are the rules against other gods, graven images, vain swearing, and Sabbath breaking. And the full text of the fifth Commandment puts forward filial respect as a condition of long life in the and "which the Lord they God giveth thee." These "[w]ords . . . make [the] . . . religious meaning unmistakably clear." *County of Allegheny v. American Civil Liberties Union, Greater Pittsburgh Chapter*, 492 U.S. 573 (1989).

To drive the religious point home, and identify the message as religious to any viewer who failed to read the text, the engraved quotation is framed by religious symbols: two tablets with what appears to be ancient script on them, two Stars of David, and the superimposed Greek letters Chi and Rho as the familiar monogram of Christ. Nothing on the monument, in fact, detracts from its religious nature, and the plurality does not suggest otherwise. It would therefore be difficult to miss the point that the government of Texas is telling everyone who sees the monument to live up to a moral code because God requires it, with both code and conception of God being rightly understood as the inheritances specifically of Jews and Christians. And it is likewise unsurprising that the District Court expressly rejected Texas's argument that the State's purpose in placing the monument on the capitol grounds was related to the Commandments' role as "part of the foundation of modern secular law in Texas and elsewhere."

The monument's presentation of the Commandments with religious text emphasized and enhanced stands in contrast to any number of perfectly constitutional depictions of them, the frieze of our own Courtroom providing a good example, where the figure of Moses stands among history's great lawgivers.

While Moses holds the tablets of the Commandments showing some Hebrew text, no one looking at the lines of figures in marble relief is likely to see a religious purpose behind the assemblage or take away a religious message from it. Only one other depiction represents a religious leader, and the historical personages are mixed with symbols of moral and intellectual abstractions like Equity and Authority. Since Moses enjoys no especial prominence on the frieze, viewers can readily take him to be there as a lawgiver in the company of other lawgivers; and the viewers may just as naturally see the tablets of the Commandments (showing the later ones, forbidding things like killing and theft, but without the divine preface) as background from which the concept of law emerged, ultimately having a secular influence in the history of the Nation. Government may, of course, constitutionally call attention to this influence, and may post displays or erect monuments recounting this aspect of our history no less than any other, so long as there is a context and that context is historical. Hence, a display of the Commandments accompanied by an exposition of how they have influenced modern law would most likely be constitutionally unobjectionable. And the Decalogue could, as *Stone* suggested, be integrated constitutionally into a course of study in public schools.

Texas seeks to take advantage of the recognition that visual symbol and written text can manifest a secular purpose in secular company, when it argues that its monument (like Moses in the frieze) is not alone and ought to be viewed as only 1 among 17 placed on the 22 acres surrounding the state capitol. Texas, indeed, says that the Capitol grounds are like a museum for a collection of exhibits, the kind of setting that several Members of the Court have said can render the exhibition of religious artifacts permissible, even though in other circumstances their display would be seen as meant to convey a religious message forbidden to the State. So, for example, the Government of the United States does not violate the Establishment Clause by hanging Giotto's Madonna on the wall of the National Gallery.

But 17 monuments with no common appearance, history, or aesthetic role scattered over 22 acres is not a museum, and anyone strolling around the lawn would surely take each memorial on its own terms without any dawning sense that some purpose held the miscellany together more coherently than fortuity and the edge of the grass. One monument expresses admiration for pioneer women. One pays respect to the fighters of World War II. And one quotes the God of Abraham whose command is the sanction for moral law. The themes are individual grit, patriotic courage, and God as the source of Jewish and Christian morality; there is no common denominator.

If the State's museum argument does nothing to blunt the religious message and manifestly religious purpose behind it, neither does the plurality's reliance on generalities culled from cases factually different from this one. In fact, it is not until the end of its opinion that the plurality turns to the relevant precedent of Stone, a case actually dealing with a display of the Decalogue.

When the plurality finally does confront *Stone*, it tries to avoid the case's obvious applicability by limiting its holding to the classroom setting. . . . I would reverse the judgment of the Court of Appeals.

□ *Justice STEVENS, with whom Justice GINSBURG joins, dissenting.*

The sole function of the monument on the grounds of Texas's State Capitol is to display the full text of one version of the Ten Commandments. The monument is not a work of art and does not refer to any event in the history of the State. It is significant because, and only because, it communicates the following message:

> "I AM the LORD thy God.
> "Thou shalt have no other gods before me.
> "Thou shalt not make to thyself any graven images.
> "Thou shalt not take the Name of the Lord thy God in vain.
> "Remember the Sabbath day, to keep it holy.
> "Honor thy father and thy mother, that thy days may be long upon the land which the Lord thy God giveth thee.
> "Thou shalt not kill.
> "Thou shalt not commit adultery.
> "Thou shalt not steal.
> "Thou shalt not bear false witness against thy neighbor.
> "Thou shalt not covet thy neighbor's house.
> "Thou shalt not covet thy neighbor's wife, nor his manservant, nor his maidservant, nor his cattle, nor anything that is thy neighbor's."

Viewed on its face, Texas's display has no purported connection to God's role in the formation of Texas or the founding of our Nation; nor does it provide the reasonable observer with any basis to guess that it was erected to honor any individual or organization. The message transmitted by Texas's chosen display is quite plain: This State endorses the divine code of the "Judeo-Christian" God.

For those of us who learned to recite the King James version of the text long before we understood the meaning of some of its words, God's Commandments may seem like wise counsel. The question before this Court, however, is whether it is counsel that the State of Texas may proclaim without violating the Establishment Clause of the Constitution. If any fragment of Jefferson's metaphorical "wall of separation between church and State" is to be preserved—if there remains any meaning to the "wholesome 'neutrality' of which this Court's [Establishment Clause] cases speak," *School Dist. of Abington Township v. Schempp*, 374 U.S. 203 (1963)—a negative answer to that question is mandatory.

In my judgment, at the very least, the Establishment Clause has created a strong presumption against the display of religious symbols on public property. The adornment of our public spaces with displays of religious symbols and messages undoubtedly provides comfort, even inspiration, to many individuals who subscribe to particular faiths. Unfortunately, the practice also runs the risk of "offend[ing] nonmembers of the faith being advertised as well as adherents who consider the particular advertisement disrespectful."

Government's obligation to avoid divisiveness and exclusion in the religious sphere is compelled by the Establishment and Free Exercise Clauses, which together erect a wall of separation between church and state. This metaphorical wall protects principles long recognized and often recited in this Court's cases. The first and most fundamental of these principles, one that a majority of this Court today affirms, is that the Establishment Clause demands religious neutrality—government may not exercise a preference for one religious faith over another. This essential command, however, is not merely a prohibition against the government's differentiation among religious sects. We have repeatedly reaffirmed that neither a State nor the Federal Government "can constitutionally pass laws or impose requirements which aid all religions as against non-believers, and neither can aid those religions based on a belief in the existence of God as against those religions founded on different beliefs." *Torcaso v. Watkins*, 367 U.S. 488 (1961). This principle is based on the straightforward notion that governmental promotion of orthodoxy is not saved by the aggregation of several orthodoxies under the State's banner. . . .

The monolith displayed on Texas Capitol grounds cannot be discounted as a passive acknowledgment of religion, nor can the State's refusal to remove it upon objection be explained as a simple desire to preserve a historic relic. This Nation's resolute commitment to neutrality with respect to religion is flatly inconsistent with the plurality's wholehearted validation of an official state endorsement of the message that there is one, and only one, God.

When the Ten Commandments monument was donated to the State of Texas in 1961, it was not for the purpose of commemorating a noteworthy event in Texas history, signifying the Commandments' influence on the development of secular law, or even denoting the religious beliefs of Texans at that time. To the contrary, the donation was only one of over a hundred largely identical monoliths, and of over a thousand paper replicas, distributed to state and local governments throughout the Nation over the course of several decades. This ambitious project was the work of the Fraternal Order of Eagles, a well-respected benevolent organization whose good works have earned the praise of several Presidents.

As the story goes, the program was initiated by the late Judge E. J. Ruegemer, a Minnesota juvenile court judge and then-Chairman of the Eagles National Commission on Youth Guidance. Inspired by a juvenile offender who had never heard of the Ten Commandments, the judge approached the Minnesota Eagles with the idea of distributing paper copies of the Commandments to be posted in courthouses nationwide. The State's Aerie undertook this project and its popularity spread. When Cecil B. DeMille, who at that time was filming the movie *The Ten Commandments*, heard of the judge's endeavor, he teamed up with the Eagles to produce the type of granite monolith now displayed in front of the Texas Capitol and at courthouse squares, city halls, and public parks throughout the Nation. Granite was reportedly chosen over DeMille's original suggestion of bronze plaques to better replicate the original Ten Commandments.

The donors were motivated by a desire to "inspire the youth" and curb juvenile delinquency by providing children with a "code of conduct or standards by which to govern their actions." It is the Eagles' belief that disseminating the message conveyed by the Ten Commandments will help to persuade young men and women to observe civilized standards of behavior, and will lead to more productive lives. Significantly, although the Eagles' organization is nonsectarian, eligibility for membership is premised on a belief in the existence of a "Supreme Being."

The desire to combat juvenile delinquency by providing guidance to youths is both admirable and unquestionably secular. But achieving that goal through biblical teachings injects a religious purpose into an otherwise secular endeavor. By spreading the word of God and converting heathens to Christianity, missionaries expect to enlighten their converts, enhance their satisfaction with life, and improve their behavior. Similarly, by disseminating the "law of God"—directing fidelity to God and proscribing murder, theft, and adultery—the Eagles hope that this divine guidance will help wayward youths conform their behavior and improve their lives. In my judgment, the significant secular by-products that are intended consequences of religious instruction—indeed, of the establishment of most religions—are not the type of "secular" purposes that justify government promulgation of sacred religious messages. . . .

The judgment of the Court in this case stands for the proposition that the Constitution permits governmental displays of sacred religious texts. This makes a mockery of the constitutional ideal that government must remain neutral between religion and irreligion. If a State may endorse a particular deity's command to "have no other gods before me," it is difficult to conceive of any textual display that would run afoul of the Establishment Clause. . . . I respectfully dissent.

McCreary v. American Civil Liberties Union of Kentucky

125 S.Ct. 2722 (2005)

Two Kentucky counties, McCreary and Pulaski, in 1999 had installed in their courthouses large copies of the King James version of the Ten

Commandments. The constitutionality of those public displays was immediately challenged by the American Civil Liberties Union (ACLU) chapter in the state. Subsequently, the counties passed resolutions declaring the Ten Commandments a "precedent legal code" for Kentucky's laws, and directing the addition of other historical documents, such as President Abraham Lincoln's declaration of a national prayer in 1863. After a federal district court found that display to run afoul of the First Amendment in 2000, the counties added several other secular documents, including the Magna Carta and the lyrics of "The Star Spangled Banner." That third display of the Ten Commandments, surrounded by other historical documents, was again challenged by the ACLU. In 2000, a district court ordered the removal of the displays. The counties appealed, arguing that the displays had a secular and educational purpose, but the Court of Appeals for the Sixth Circuit disagreed and affirmed the trial court. Whereupon, McCreary county appealed and the Supreme Court granted review.

The appellate court's decision was affirmed on a five to four vote. Justice Souter delivered the opinion for the Court. Justice O'Connor filed a concurring opinion. Justice Scalia filed a dissenting opinion, which Chief Justice Rehnquist and Justices Kennedy and Thomas joined.

□ *Justice SOUTER delivered the opinion of the Court.*

Twenty-five years ago in a case prompted by posting the Ten Commandments in Kentucky's public schools, this Court recognized that the Commandments "are undeniably a sacred text in the Jewish and Christian faiths" and held that their display in public classrooms violated the First Amendment's bar against establishment of religion. *Stone* [*v. Graham*] 449 U.S. [39 (1980)]. *Stone* found a predominantly religious purpose in the government's posting of the Commandments, given their prominence as "'an instrument of religion'" (quoting *School Dist. of Abington Township v. Schempp*, 374 U.S. 203 (1963)). The Counties ask for a different approach here by arguing that official purpose is unknowable and the search for it inherently vain. In the alternative, the Counties would avoid the District Court's conclusion by having us limit the scope of the purpose enquiry so severely that any trivial rationalization would suffice, under a standard oblivious to the history of religious government action like the progression of exhibits in this case.

Ever since *Lemon v. Kurtzman* [403 U.S. 602 (1971)] summarized the three familiar considerations for evaluating Establishment Clause claims, looking to whether government action has "a secular legislative purpose" has been a common, albeit seldom dispositive, element of our cases. Though we have found government action motivated by an illegitimate purpose only four times since *Lemon*, and "the secular purpose requirement alone may rarely be determinative . . . , it nevertheless serves an important function." *Wallace v. Jaffree*, 472 U.S. 38 (1985) (O'CONNOR, J., concurring in judgment).

The touchstone for our analysis is the principle that the "First Amendment mandates governmental neutrality between religion and religion, and between religion and nonreligion." *Epperson v. Arkansas*, 393 U.S. 97 (1968);

Everson v. Board of Ed. of Ewing, 330 U.S. 1 (1947); *Wallace v. Jaffree.* When the government acts with the ostensible and predominant purpose of advancing religion, it violates that central Establishment Clause value of official religious neutrality, there being no neutrality when the government's ostensible object is to take sides.

Indeed, the purpose apparent from government action can have an impact more significant than the result expressly decreed: when the government maintains Sunday closing laws, it advances religion only minimally because many working people would take the day as one of rest regardless, but if the government justified its decision with a stated desire for all Americans to honor Christ, the divisive thrust of the official action would be inescapable. This is the teaching of *McGowan v. Maryland*, 366 U.S. 420 (1961), which upheld Sunday closing statutes on practical, secular grounds after finding that the government had forsaken the religious purposes behind centuries-old predecessor laws.

Despite the intuitive importance of official purpose to the realization of Establishment Clause values, the Counties ask us to abandon *Lemon*'s purpose test, or at least to truncate any enquiry into purpose here. Their first argument is that the very consideration of purpose is deceptive: according to them, true "purpose" is unknowable, and its search merely an excuse for courts to act selectively and unpredictably in picking out evidence of subjective intent. The assertions are as seismic as they are unconvincing.

Examination of purpose is a staple of statutory interpretation that makes up the daily fare of every appellate court in the country, and governmental purpose is a key element of a good deal of constitutional doctrine, *Church of Lukumi Babalu Aye, Inc. v. Hialeah*, 508 U.S. 520 (1993) (discriminatory purpose raises level of scrutiny required by free exercise claim). With enquiries into purpose this common, if they were nothing but hunts for mares' nests deflecting attention from bare judicial will, the whole notion of purpose in law would have dropped into disrepute long ago.

But scrutinizing purpose does make practical sense, as in Establishment Clause analysis, where an understanding of official objective emerges from readily discoverable fact, without any judicial psychoanalysis of a drafter's heart of hearts. The eyes that look to purpose belong to an "'objective observer,'" one who takes account of the traditional external signs that show up in the "'text, legislative history, and implementation of the statute,'" or comparable official act. There is, then, nothing hinting at an unpredictable or disingenuous exercise when a court enquires into purpose after a claim is raised under the Establishment Clause.

The cases with findings of a predominantly religious purpose point to the straightforward nature of the test. In *Wallace*, for example, we inferred purpose from a change of wording from an earlier statute to a later one, each dealing with prayer in schools. . . .

After declining the invitation to abandon concern with purpose wholesale, we also have to avoid the Counties' alternative tack of trivializing the enquiry into it. The Counties would read the cases as if the purpose enquiry were so naive that any transparent claim to secularity would satisfy it, and they would cut context out of the enquiry, to the point of ignoring history, no matter what bearing it actually had on the significance of current circumstances. There is no precedent for the Counties' arguments, or reason supporting them.

Lemon said that government action must have "a secular . . . purpose," and after a host of cases it is fair to add that although a legislature's stated reasons will generally get deference, the secular purpose required has to be genuine, not a sham, and not merely secondary to a religious objective. . . .

We take *Stone* as the initial legal benchmark, our only case dealing with the constitutionality of displaying the Commandments. *Stone* recognized that the Commandments are an "instrument of religion" and that, at least on the facts before it, the display of their text could presumptively be understood as meant to advance religion: although state law specifically required their posting in public school classrooms, their isolated exhibition did not leave room even for an argument that secular education explained their being there. But *Stone* did not purport to decide the constitutionality of every possible way the Commandments might be set out by the government, and under the Establishment Clause detail is key. *County of Allegheny v. American Civil Liberties Union, Greater Pittsburgh Chapter*, 492 U.S. 573 (1989) (opinion of BLACKMUN, J.) ("[T]he question is what viewers may fairly understand to be the purpose of the display. That inquiry, of necessity, turns upon the context in which the contested object appears"). Hence, we look to the record of evidence showing the progression leading up to the third display of the Commandments.

The display rejected in *Stone* had two obvious similarities to the first one in the sequence here: both set out a text of the Commandments as distinct from any traditionally symbolic representation, and each stood alone, not part of an arguably secular display. *Stone* stressed the significance of integrating the Commandments into a secular scheme to forestall the broadcast of an otherwise clearly religious message, and for good reason, the Commandments being a central point of reference in the religious and moral history of Jews and Christians. They proclaim the existence of a monotheistic god (no other gods). . . . The reasonable observer could only think that the Counties meant to emphasize and celebrate the Commandments' religious message.

This is not to deny that the Commandments have had influence on civil or secular law; a major text of a majority religion is bound to be felt. The point is simply that the original text viewed in its entirety is an unmistakably religious statement dealing with religious obligations and with morality subject to religious sanction. When the government initiates an effort to place this statement alone in public view, a religious object is unmistakable.

Once the Counties were sued, they modified the exhibits and invited additional insight into their purpose in a display that hung for about six months. This new one was the product of forthright and nearly identical Pulaski and McCreary County resolutions listing a series of American historical documents with theistic and Christian references, which were to be posted in order to furnish a setting for displaying the Ten Commandments and any "other Kentucky and American historical documen[t]" without raising concern about "any Christian or religious references" in them. As mentioned, the resolutions expressed support for an Alabama judge who posted the Commandments in his courtroom, and cited the fact the Kentucky Legislature once adjourned a session in honor of "Jesus Christ, Prince of Ethics."

In this second display, unlike the first, the Commandments were not hung in isolation, merely leaving the Counties' purpose to emerge from the pervasively religious text of the Commandments themselves. Instead, the second version was required to include the statement of the government's purpose expressly set out in the county resolutions, and underscored it by juxtaposing the Commandments to other documents with highlighted references to God as their sole common element. The display's unstinting focus was on religious passages, showing that the Counties were posting the Commandments precisely because of their sectarian content. That demonstration of the government's objective was enhanced by serial religious references and the accompanying resolution's claim about the embodiment of ethics in Christ. Together, the display and resolution presented an indisputable, and undisputed, showing of an impermissible purpose.

Today, the Counties make no attempt to defend their undeniable objective, but instead hopefully describe version two as "dead and buried." Their refusal to defend the second display is understandable, but the reasonable observer could not forget it. After the Counties changed lawyers, they mounted a third display, without a new resolution or repeal of the old one. The result was the "Foundations of American Law and Government" exhibit, which placed the Commandments in the company of other documents the Counties thought especially significant in the historical foundation of American government. In trying to persuade the District Court to lift the preliminary injunction, the Counties cited several new purposes for the third version, including a desire "to educate the citizens of the county regarding some of the documents that played a significant role in the foundation of our system of law and government." The Counties' claims did not, however, persuade the court, intimately familiar with the details of this litigation, or the Court of Appeals, neither of which found a legitimizing secular purpose in this third version of the display. The conclusions of the two courts preceding us in this case are well warranted.

These new statements of purpose were presented only as a litigating position, there being no further authorizing action by the Counties' governing boards. And although repeal of the earlier county authorizations would not have erased them from the record of evidence bearing on current purpose, the extraordinary resolutions for the second display passed just months earlier were not repealed or otherwise repudiated. Indeed, the sectarian spirit of the common resolution found enhanced expression in the third display, which quoted more of the purely religious language of the Commandments than the first two displays had done ("I the LORD thy God am a jealous God") (text of Second Commandment in third display); ("the LORD will not hold him guiltless that taketh his name in vain") (from text of Third Commandment); and ("that thy days may be long upon the land which the LORD thy God giveth thee") (text of Fifth Commandment). No reasonable observer could swallow the claim that the Counties had cast off the objective so unmistakable in the earlier displays.

Nor did the selection of posted material suggest a clear theme that might prevail over evidence of the continuing religious object. In a collection of documents said to be "foundational" to American government, it is at least odd to include a patriotic anthem, but to omit the Fourteenth Amendment, the most significant structural provision adopted since the original Framing. . . .

In holding the preliminary injunction adequately supported by evidence that the Counties' purpose had not changed at the third stage, we do not decide that the Counties' past actions forever taint any effort on their part to deal with the subject matter. We hold only that purpose needs to be taken seriously under the Establishment Clause and needs to be understood in light of context; an implausible claim that governmental purpose has changed should not carry the day in a court of law any more than in a head with common sense. . . .

Nor do we have occasion here to hold that a sacred text can never be integrated constitutionally into a governmental display on the subject of law, or American history. We do not forget, and in this litigation have frequently been reminded, that our own courtroom frieze was deliberately designed in the exercise of governmental authority so as to include the figure of Moses holding tablets exhibiting a portion of the Hebrew text of the later, secularly phrased Commandments; in the company of 17 other lawgivers, most of them secular figures, there is no risk that Moses would strike an observer as evidence that the National Government was violating neutrality in religion.

The importance of neutrality as an interpretive guide is no less true now than it was when the Court broached the principle in *Everson v. Board of Ed. of Ewing*, 330 U.S. 1 (1947), and a word needs to be said about the different view taken in today's dissent. We all agree, of course, on the need for some interpretative help. The First Amendment contains no textual definition of "establishment," and the term is certainly not self-defining. No one contends that the prohibition of establishment stops at a designation of a national (or with Fourteenth Amendment incorporation, *Cantwell v. Connecticut*, 310 U.S. 296 (1940), a state) church, but nothing in the text says just how much more it covers. There is no simple answer, for more than one reason.

The prohibition on establishment covers a variety of issues from prayer in widely varying government settings, to financial aid for religious individuals and institutions, to comment on religious questions. In these varied settings, issues of about interpreting inexact Establishment Clause language, like difficult interpretative issues generally, arise from the tension of competing values, each constitutionally respectable, but none open to realization to the logical limit. . . .

Given the variety of interpretative problems, the principle of neutrality has provided a good sense of direction: the government may not favor one religion over another, or religion over irreligion, religious choice being the prerogative of individuals under the Free Exercise Clause. The principle has been helpful simply because it responds to one of the major concerns that prompted adoption of the Religion Clauses. The Framers and the citizens of their time intended not only to protect the integrity of individual conscience in religious matters, *Wallace v. Jaffree*, but to guard against the civic divisiveness that follows when the Government weighs in on one side of religious debate; nothing does a better job of roiling society, a point that needed no explanation to the descendants of English Puritans and Cavaliers (or Massachusetts Puritans and Baptists). A sense of the past thus points to governmental neutrality as an objective of the Establishment Clause, and a sensible standard for applying it. To be sure, given its generality as a principle, an appeal to neutrality alone cannot possibly lay every issue to rest, or tell us what issues on the margins are substantial enough for constitutional significance, a point that has been clear from the Founding era to modern times. But invoking neutrality is a prudent way of keeping sight of something the Framers of the First Amendment thought important. . . .

[W]e affirm the Sixth Circuit in upholding the preliminary injunction.

□ *Justice O'CONNOR, concurring.*

Reasonable minds can disagree about how to apply the Religion Clauses in a given case. But the goal of the Clauses is clear: to carry out the Founders' plan of preserving religious liberty to the fullest extent possible in a pluralistic society. By enforcing the Clauses, we have kept religion a matter for the individual conscience, not for the prosecutor or bureaucrat. At a time when we see around the world the violent consequences of the assumption of religious authority by government, Americans may count themselves fortunate: Our regard for constitutional boundaries has protected us from similar travails, while allowing private religious exercise to flourish. The well-known statement that "[w]e are a religious people," *Zorach v. Clauson*, 343 U.S. 306 (1952), has proved true. Americans attend their places of worship more often than do citizens of other developed nations, and describe religion as playing an especially important role in their lives. Those who would renegotiate the boundaries between church and state must therefore answer a difficult question: Why would we trade a system that has served us so well for one that has served others so poorly?

Our guiding principle has been James Madison's—that "[t]he Religion . . . of every man must be left to the conviction and conscience of every man." *Memorial and Remonstrance Against Religious Assessments.* To that end, we have held that the guarantees of religious freedom protect citizens from religious incursions by the States as well as by the Federal Government. Government may not coerce a person into worshiping against her will, nor prohibit her from worshiping according to it. It may not prefer one religion over another or promote religion over nonbelief. It may not entangle itself with religion. And government may not, by "endorsing religion or a religious practice," "mak[e] adherence to religion relevant to a person's standing in the political community." *Wallace v. Jaffree*, 472 U.S. 38 (1985).

When we enforce these restrictions, we do so for the same reason that guided the Framers—respect for religion's special role in society. Our Founders conceived of a Republic receptive to voluntary religious expression, and provided for the possibility of judicial intervention when government action threatens or impedes such expression. Voluntary religious belief and expression may be as threatened when government takes the mantle of religion upon itself as when government directly interferes with private religious practices. When the government associates one set of religious beliefs with the state and identifies nonadherents as outsiders, it encroaches upon the individual's decision about whether and how to worship. In the marketplace of ideas, the government has vast resources and special status. Government religious expression therefore risks crowding out private observance and distorting the natural interplay between competing beliefs. Allowing government to be a potential mouthpiece for competing religious ideas risks the sort of division that might easily spill over into suppression of rival beliefs. Tying secular and religious authority together poses risks to both.

Given the history of this particular display of the Ten Commandments, the Court correctly finds an Establishment Clause violation. The purpose behind the counties' display is relevant because it conveys an unmistakable message of endorsement to the reasonable observer. . . .

In my opinion, the display at issue was an establishment of religion in violation of our Constitution. For the reasons given above, I join in the Court's opinion.

□ *Justice SCALIA, with whom THE CHIEF JUSTICE and Justice THOMAS join, and with whom Justice KENNEDY joins [in part], dissenting.*

[O]ne model of the relationship between church and state—a model spread across Europe by the armies of Napoleon, and reflected in the Constitution of France, which begins "France is [a] . . . secular . . . Republic." Religion is to be strictly excluded from the public forum. This is not, and never was, the model adopted by America. George Washington added to the form of Presidential oath prescribed by Art. II, Sec. 1, cl. 8, of the Constitution, the concluding words "so help me God." The Supreme Court under JOHN MARSHALL opened its sessions with the prayer, "God save the United States and this Honorable Court." The First Congress instituted the practice of beginning its legislative sessions with a prayer. *Marsh v. Chambers*, 463 U.S. 783 (1983). The same week that Congress submitted the Establishment Clause as part of the Bill of Rights for ratification by the States, it enacted legislation providing for paid chaplains in the House and Senate. The day after the First Amendment was proposed, the same Congress that had proposed it requested the President to proclaim "a day of public thanksgiving and prayer, to be observed, by acknowledging, with grateful hearts, the many and signal favours of Almighty God." President Washington offered the first Thanksgiving Proclamation shortly thereafter, devoting November 26, 1789, on behalf of the American people "'to the service of that great and glorious Being who is the beneficent author of all the good that is, that was, or that will be,'" thus beginning a tradition of offering gratitude to God that continues today. The same Congress also reenacted the Northwest Territory Ordinance of 1787, 1 Stat. 50, Article III of which provided: "Religion, morality, and knowledge, being necessary to good government and the happiness of mankind, schools and the means of education shall forever be encouraged." And of course the First Amendment itself accords religion (and no other manner of belief) special constitutional protection.

These actions of our First President and Congress and the MARSHALL Court were not idiosyncratic; they reflected the beliefs of the period. Those who wrote the Constitution believed that morality was essential to the well-being of society and that encouragement of religion was the best way to foster morality. . . .

Nor have the views of our people on this matter significantly changed. Presidents continue to conclude the Presidential oath with the words "so help me God." Our legislatures, state and national, continue to open their sessions with prayer led by official chaplains. The sessions of this Court continue to open with the prayer "God save the United States and this Honorable Court." Invocation of the Almighty by our public figures, at all levels of government, remains commonplace. Our coinage bears the motto "IN GOD WE TRUST." And our Pledge of Allegiance contains the acknowledgment that we are a Nation "under God." As one of our Supreme Court opinions rightly observed, "We are a religious people whose institutions presuppose a Supreme Being." *Zorach v. Clauson*, 343 U.S. 306 (1952), repeated with approval in *Lynch v. Donnelly*, 465 U.S. 668 (1984).

With all of this reality (and much more) staring it in the face, how can the Court possibly assert that "'the First Amendment mandates governmental neutrality between . . . religion and nonreligion,'" and that "[m]anifesting a purpose to favor . . . adherence to religion generally," is unconstitutional? Who says so? Surely not the words of the Constitution. Surely not the history and traditions that reflect our society's constant understanding of those words. Surely not even the current sense of our society. . . . Nothing stands behind the Court's assertion that governmental affirmation of the society's belief in God is unconstitutional except the Court's own say-so, citing as support only the unsubstantiated say-so of earlier Courts going back no farther than the mid-20th century. . . .

What distinguishes the rule of law from the dictatorship of a shifting Supreme Court majority is the absolutely indispensable requirement that judicial opinions be grounded in consistently applied principle. That is what prevents judges from ruling now this way, now that—thumbs up or thumbs down—as their personal preferences dictate. Today's opinion forthrightly (or actually, somewhat less than forthrightly) admits that it does not rest upon consistently applied principle. In a revealing footnote, the Court acknowledges that the "Establishment Clause doctrine" it purports to be applying "lacks the comfort of categorical absolutes." What the Court means by this lovely euphemism is that sometimes the Court chooses to decide cases on the principle that government cannot favor religion, and sometimes it does not. The footnote goes on to say that "[i]n special instances we have found good reason" to dispense with the principle, but "[n]o such reasons present themselves here." It does not identify all of those "special instances," much less identify the "good reason" for their existence. . . .

Besides appealing to the demonstrably false principle that the government cannot favor religion over irreligion, today's opinion suggests that the posting of the Ten Commandments violates the principle that the government cannot favor one religion over another. That is indeed a valid principle where public aid or assistance to religion is concerned, see *Zelman v. Simmons-Harris*, 536 U.S. 639 (2002), or where the free exercise of religion is at issue, *Church of Lukumi Babalu Aye, Inc. v. Hialeah*, 508 U.S. 520 (1993), but it necessarily applies in a more limited sense to public acknowledgment of the Creator. If religion in the public forum had to be entirely nondenominational, there could be no religion in the public forum at all. One cannot say the word "God," or "the Almighty," one cannot offer public supplication or thanksgiving, without contradicting the beliefs of some people that there are many gods, or that God or the gods pay no attention to human affairs. With respect to public acknowledgment of religious belief, it is entirely clear from our Nation's historical practices that the Establishment Clause permits this disregard of polytheists and believers in unconcerned deities, just as it permits the disregard of devout atheists. The Thanksgiving Proclamation issued by George Washington at the instance of the First Congress was scrupulously nondenominational—but it was monotheistic. In *Marsh v. Chambers*, we said that the fact the particular prayers offered in the Nebraska Legislature were "in the Judeo-Christian tradition," posed no additional problem, because "there is no indication that the prayer opportunity has been exploited to proselytize or advance any one, or to disparage any other, faith or belief."

Historical practices thus demonstrate that there is a distance between the acknowledgment of a single Creator and the establishment of a religion. The former is, as *Marsh v. Chambers* put it, "a tolerable acknowledgment of beliefs widely held among the people of this country." The three most popular religions in the United States, Christianity, Judaism, and Islam—which combined account for 97.7% of all believers—are monotheistic. All of them, moreover (Islam included), believe that the Ten Commandments were given by God to Moses, and are divine prescriptions for a virtuous life. Publicly honoring the Ten Commandments is thus indistinguishable, insofar as discriminating against other religions is concerned, from publicly honoring God. . . .

To any person who happened to walk down the hallway of the McCreary or Pulaski County Courthouse during the roughly nine months when the Foundations Displays were exhibited, the displays must have seemed unremarkable—if indeed they were noticed at all. The walls of both courthouses were already lined with historical documents and other assorted portraits; each Foundations Display was exhibited in the same format as these other displays and nothing in the record suggests that either County took steps to give it greater prominence.

Entitled "The Foundations of American Law and Government Display," each display consisted of nine equally sized documents: the original version of the Magna Carta, the Declaration of Independence, the Bill of Rights, the Star Spangled Banner, the Mayflower Compact of 1620, a picture of Lady Justice, the National Motto of the United States ("In God We Trust"), the Preamble to the Kentucky Constitution, and the Ten Commandments. The displays did not emphasize any of the nine documents in any way: The frame holding the Ten Commandments was of the same size and had the same appearance as that which held each of the other documents.

Posted with the documents was a plaque, identifying the display, and explaining that it "contains documents that played a significant role in the foundation of our system of law and government." [T]he Foundations Displays manifested the purely secular purpose that the Counties asserted before the District Court: "to display documents that played a significant role in the foundation of our system of law and government." That the Displays included the Ten Commandments did not transform their apparent secular purpose into one of impermissible advocacy for Judeo-Christian beliefs. . . .

Acknowledgment of the contribution that religion has made to our Nation's legal and governmental heritage partakes of a centuries-old tradition. . . .

Perhaps in recognition of the centrality of the Ten Commandments as a widely recognized symbol of religion in public life, the Court is at pains to dispel the impression that its decision will require governments across the country to sandblast the Ten Commandments from the public square. The constitutional problem, the Court says, is with the Counties' purpose in erecting the Foundations Displays, not the displays themselves. The Court adds in a footnote: "One consequence of taking account of the purpose underlying past actions is that the same government action may be constitutional if taken in the first instance and unconstitutional if it has a sectarian heritage."

This inconsistency may be explicable in theory, but I suspect that the "objective observer" with whom the Court is so concerned will recognize its absurdity in practice. By virtue of details familiar only to the parties to litigation and their lawyers, McCreary and Pulaski Counties, Kentucky, and Rutherford County, Tennessee, have been ordered to remove the same display that appears in courthouses from Mercer County, Kentucky to Elkhart County, Indiana. Displays erected in silence (and under the direction of good legal advice) are permissible, while those hung after discussion and debate are deemed unconstitutional. Reduction of the Establishment Clause to such minutiae trivializes the Clause's protection against religious establishment; indeed, it may inflame religious passions by making the passing comments of every government official the subject of endless litigation. . . .

In sum: The first displays did not necessarily evidence an intent to further religious practice; nor did the second displays, or the resolutions authorizing them; and there is in any event no basis for attributing whatever intent motivated the first and second displays to the third. Given the presumption of regularity that always accompanies our review of official action, the Court has identified no evidence of a purpose to advance religion in a way that is inconsistent with our cases. The Court may well be correct in identifying the third displays as the fruit of a desire to display the Ten Commandments, ante, at 24, but neither our cases nor our history support its assertion that such a desire renders the fruit poisonous.

For the foregoing reasons, I would reverse the judgment of the Court of Appeals.

B | *Free Exercise of Religion*

In its 2005-2006 term, the Court will reconsider the constitutionality of the 1993 Religious Freedom Restoration Act (RFRA), which provides that government may not "substantially burden a person's exercise of religion" unless it uses the least drastic means to achieve a "compelling goal." The RFRA was enacted in order to override the ruling in *Oregon v. Smith*, 494 U.S. 872 (1990) (excerpted in Vol. II, Ch. 6). But subsequently, in *City of Boerne v. Flores*, 521 U.S. 507 (1997) (excerpted in Vol. II, Ch. 6), the Court ruled that the RFRA does not apply to state and local laws because Congress exceeded its powers. At issue in *Gonzales v. O Centro Espirita Beneficiente Unaio do Vegetal* (No. 04-1084) is whether a lower court erred in holding that the RFRA bars the enforcement of federal laws against the importation of hallucinogens for use in a church's rituals. The church claims that it has a right to import *hoasca*, a psychedelic substance brewed in tea, for certain religious rituals. The Bush administration counters that the importation of *hoasca* violates drug-control laws and the 1971 U.N. Convention on Psychotropic Substances, which binds the government to battling international trafficking in hallucinogens.

7

The Fourth Amendment Guarantee Against Unreasonable Searches and Seizures

A | *Requirements for a Warrant and Reasonable Searches and Seizures*

In *Muehler v. Mena*, 125 S.Ct. 1465 (2005), the Court held unanimously that when executing a search warrant police may handcuff and detain the occupants in order to minimize the risk of harm to the officers. Writing for the Court, Chief Justice Rehnquist reaffirmed the holding in *Michigan v. Summers*, 452 U.S. 692 (1981), that police executing a warrant for contraband may "detain the occupants of the premises while a proper search is conducted."

In its 2005-2006 term the Court will consider, in *Georgia v. Randolph* (No. 04-1067), whether police may search a home without a warrant based on the consent of one spouse and over the objections of the other. The Georgia state supreme court held that when both spouses are present they both must consent to a warrantless police search of their premises.

B | *Exceptions to the Warrant Requirement*

Illinois v. Caballes

125 S.CT. 834 (2005)

Illinois state trooper Daniel Gillette stopped Roy Caballes for speeding and radioed the police dispatcher to report the stop. A second trooper, Craig Graham overheard the transmission and immediately headed for the scene with his narcotics-detection dog. When they arrived, while Gillette was writing a ticket, Graham walked his dog around Caballes's car. The dog alerted at the trunk and the officers searched the trunk, found marijuana, and arrested Caballes. The entire incident lasted less than ten minutes. Caballes was convicted of a narcotics offense and sentenced to twelve years' imprisonment and a $256,136 fine. The trial judge denied Caballes's motion to suppress the seized evidence and held that the officers had not unnecessarily prolonged the stop and that the dog alert was sufficiently reliable to provide probable cause to conduct the search. Although an appellate court affirmed, the Illinois Supreme Court reversed, concluding that because the canine sniff was performed without any "'specific and articulable facts'" to suggest drug activity, the use of the dog "unjustifiably enlarg[ed] the scope of a routine traffic stop into a drug investigation." The state appealed that decision and the Supreme Court granted review.

The state supreme court's decision was reversed by a vote of six to two, with Chief Justice Rehnquist not participating. Justice Stevens delivered the opinion for the Court. Justices Souter and Ginsburg each filed dissenting opinions.

□ *Justice STEVENS delivered the opinion of the Court.*

The question on which we granted *certiorari* is narrow: "Whether the Fourth Amendment requires reasonable, articulable suspicion to justify using a drug-detection dog to sniff a vehicle during a legitimate traffic stop." . . . Here, the initial seizure of respondent when he was stopped on the highway was based on probable cause, and was concededly lawful. It is nevertheless clear that a seizure that is lawful at its inception can violate the Fourth Amendment if its manner of execution unreasonably infringes interests protected by the Constitution. A seizure that is justified solely by the interest in issuing a warning ticket to the driver can become unlawful if it is prolonged beyond the time reasonably required to complete that mission. . . .

Official conduct that does not "compromise any legitimate interest in privacy" is not a search subject to the Fourth Amendment. We have held that any interest in possessing contraband cannot be deemed "legitimate," and thus, governmental conduct that only reveals the possession of contraband "compromises no legitimate privacy interest." This is because the expectation "that certain facts will not come to the attention of the authorities" is not the same as an interest in "privacy that society is prepared to consider reasonable." In *United States v. Place*, 462 U.S. 696 (1983), we treated a canine sniff by a well-trained narcotics-detection dog as "*sui generis*" because it "discloses only the presence or absence of narcotics, a contraband item." . . .

Accordingly, the use of a well-trained narcotics-detection dog—one that "does not expose noncontraband items that otherwise would remain hidden from public view"—during a lawful traffic stop, generally does not implicate legitimate privacy interests. In this case, the dog sniff was performed on the exterior of respondent's car while he was lawfully seized for a traffic violation. Any intrusion on respondent's privacy expectations does not rise to the level of a constitutionally cognizable infringement.

This conclusion is entirely consistent with our recent decision that the use of a thermal-imaging device to detect the growth of marijuana in a home constituted an unlawful search. *Kyllo v. United States*, 533 U.S. 27 (2001). Critical to that decision was the fact that the device was capable of detecting lawful activity—in that case, intimate details in a home, such as "at what hour each night the lady of the house takes her daily sauna and bath." The legitimate expectation that information about perfectly lawful activity will remain private is categorically distinguishable from respondent's hopes or expectations concerning the nondetection of contraband in the trunk of his car. A dog sniff conducted during a concededly lawful traffic stop that reveals no information other than the location of a substance that no individual has any right to possess does not violate the Fourth Amendment. . . .

□ *Justice SOUTER, dissenting.*

I would hold that using the dog for the purposes of determining the presence of marijuana in the car's trunk was a search unauthorized as an incident of the speeding stop and unjustified on any other ground. . . .

At the heart both of [*United States v.*] *Place*, [462 U.S. 696 (1983)], and the Court's opinion today is the proposition that sniffs by a trained dog are *sui generis* because a reaction by the dog in going alert is a response to nothing but the presence of contraband. Hence, the argument goes, because the sniff can only reveal the presence of items devoid of any legal use, the sniff "does not implicate legitimate privacy interests" and is not to be treated as a search.

The infallible dog, however, is a creature of legal fiction. Although the Supreme Court of Illinois did not get into the sniffing averages of drug dogs, their supposed infallibility is belied by judicial opinions describing well-trained animals sniffing and alerting with less than perfect accuracy, whether owing to errors by their handlers, the limitations of the dogs themselves, or even the pervasive contamination of currency by cocaine. See, e.g., *United States v. Kennedy*, 131 F.3d 1371 (CA10 1997) (describing a dog that had a 71% accuracy rate); *United States v. Scarborough*, 128 F.3d 1373 (CA10 1997) (describing a dog that erroneously alerted 4 times out of 19 while working for the postal service and 8% of the time over its entire career); *United States v. Limares*, 269 F.3d 794 (CA7 2001) (accepting as reliable a dog that gave false positives between 7 and 38% of the time). . . .

Once the dog's fallibility is recognized, however, that ends the justification claimed in *Place* for treating the sniff as sui generis under the Fourth

Amendment: the sniff alert does not necessarily signal hidden contraband, and opening the container or enclosed space whose emanations the dog has sensed will not necessarily reveal contraband or any other evidence of crime. This is not, of course, to deny that a dog's reaction may provide reasonable suspicion, or probable cause, to search the container or enclosure; the Fourth Amendment does not demand certainty of success to justify a search for evidence or contraband. The point is simply that the sniff and alert cannot claim the certainty that *Place* assumed, both in treating the deliberate use of sniffing dogs as *sui generis* and then taking that characterization as a reason to say they are not searches subject to Fourth Amendment scrutiny. And when that aura of uniqueness disappears, there is no basis in *Place*'s reasoning, and no good reason otherwise, to ignore the actual function that dog sniffs perform. They are conducted to obtain information about the contents of private spaces beyond anything that human senses could perceive, even when conventionally enhanced. The information is not provided by independent third parties beyond the reach of constitutional limitations, but gathered by the government's own officers in order to justify searches of the traditional sort, which may or may not reveal evidence of crime but will disclose anything meant to be kept private in the area searched. Thus in practice the government's use of a trained narcotics dog functions as a limited search to reveal undisclosed facts about private enclosures, to be used to justify a further and complete search of the enclosed area. And given the fallibility of the dog, the sniff is the first step in a process that may disclose "intimate details" without revealing contraband, just as a thermal-imaging device might do, as described in *Kyllo v. United States*, 533 U.S. 27 (2001).

It makes sense, then, to treat a sniff as the search that it amounts to in practice, and to rely on the body of our Fourth Amendment cases, including *Kyllo*, in deciding whether such a search is reasonable. As a general proposition, using a dog to sniff for drugs is subject to the rule that the object of enforcing criminal laws does not, without more, justify suspicionless Fourth Amendment intrusions. Since the police claim to have had no particular suspicion that Caballes was violating any drug law, this sniff search must stand or fall on its being ancillary to the traffic stop that led up to it. It is true that the police had probable cause to stop the car for an offense committed in the officer's presence, which Caballes concedes could have justified his arrest. There is no occasion to consider authority incident to arrest, however, for the police did nothing more than detain Caballes long enough to check his record and write a ticket. As a consequence, the reasonableness of the search must be assessed in relation to the actual delay the police chose to impose, and as Justice GINSBURG points out in her opinion, the Fourth Amendment consequences of stopping for a traffic citation are settled law. . . .

[I]n the case of the dog sniff, the dog does not smell the disclosed contraband; it smells a closed container. An affirmative reaction therefore does not identify a substance the police already legitimately possess, but informs the police instead merely of a reasonable chance of finding contraband they have yet to put their hands on. The police will then open the container and discover whatever lies within, be it marijuana or the owner's private papers. Thus, . . . both the certainty and the limit on disclosure that may follow are missing when the dog sniffs the car.

The Court today does not go so far as to say explicitly that sniff searches by dogs trained to sense contraband always get a free pass under the Fourth

Amendment, since it reserves judgment on the constitutional significance of sniffs assumed to be more intrusive than a dog's walk around a stopped car. . . . For the sake of providing a workable framework to analyze cases on facts like these, which are certain to come along, I would treat the dog sniff as the familiar search it is in fact, subject to scrutiny under the Fourth Amendment.

□ *Justice GINSBURG, with whom Justice SOUTER joins, dissenting.*

In *Terry v. Ohio*, [392 U.S. 1 (1968)], the Court upheld the stop and subsequent frisk of an individual based on an officer's observation of suspicious behavior and his reasonable belief that the suspect was armed. In a *Terry*-type investigatory stop, "the officer's action [must be] justified at its inception, and . . . reasonably related in scope to the circumstances which justified the interference in the first place." In applying *Terry*, the Court has several times indicated that the limitation on "scope" is not confined to the duration of the seizure; it also encompasses the manner in which the seizure is conducted. I would apply *Terry*'s reasonable-relation test, as the Illinois Supreme Court did, to determine whether the canine sniff impermissibly expanded the scope of the initially valid seizure of Caballes.

It is hardly dispositive that the dog sniff in this case may not have lengthened the duration of the stop. *Terry*, it merits repetition, instructs that any investigation must be "reasonably related in scope to the circumstances which justified the interference in the first place." The unwarranted and nonconsensual expansion of the seizure here from a routine traffic stop to a drug investigation broadened the scope of the investigation in a manner that, in my judgment, runs afoul of the Fourth Amendment. . . .

In my view, the Court diminishes the Fourth Amendment's force by abandoning the second *Terry* inquiry (was the police action "reasonably related in scope to the circumstances [justifying] the [initial] interference"). A drug-detection dog is an intimidating animal. Injecting such an animal into a routine traffic stop changes the character of the encounter between the police and the motorist. The stop becomes broader, more adversarial, and (in at least some cases) longer. Caballes—who, as far as Troopers Gillette and Graham knew, was guilty solely of driving six miles per hour over the speed limit—was exposed to the embarrassment and intimidation of being investigated, on a public thoroughfare, for drugs. Even if the drug sniff is not characterized as a Fourth Amendment "search," cf. *Indianapolis v. Edmond*, 531 U.S. 32 (2000); *United States v. Place*, 462 U.S. 696 (1983), the sniff surely broadened the scope of the traffic-violation-related seizure.

[T]oday's decision . . . clears the way for suspicionless, dog-accompanied drug sweeps of parked cars along sidewalks and in parking lots. Nor would motorists have constitutional grounds for complaint should police with dogs, stationed at long traffic lights, circle cars waiting for the red signal to turn green. . . . The dog sniff in this case, it bears emphasis, was for drug detection only. A dog sniff for explosives, involving security interests not presented here, would be an entirely different matter. Detector dogs are ordinarily trained not as all-purpose sniffers, but for discrete purposes. . . .

For the reasons stated, I would hold that the police violated Caballes's Fourth Amendment rights when, without cause to suspect wrongdoing, they conducted a dog sniff of his vehicle. I would therefore affirm the judgment of the Illinois Supreme Court.

F | *The Exclusionary Rule*

In its 2005–2006 term, the Court will revisit the "inevitable discovery" exception to the Fourth Amendment's exclusionary rule that was upheld in *Nix v. Williams*, 467 U.S. 431 (1984) (excerpted in Vol. 2, Ch. 7). *Hudson v. Michigan* (No. 04-1360) poses the question of whether the "inevitable discovery" doctrine creates a per se exception to the exclusionary rule for evidence seized after a violation of the "knock and announce" rule of the Fourth Amendment for when police enter a home.

9

The Rights to Counsel and Other Procedural Guarantees

B | *Plea Bargaining and the Right to Effective Counsel*

■ The Development of Law

Rulings on Plea Bargaining and Effective Counsel

CASE	VOTE	RULING
Florida v. Nixon, 125 S.Ct. 551 (2004)	8:0	Writing for the Court, Justice Ginsburg held that the Sixth Amendment by an attorney's confessing his client's guilt in a gruesome murder case, without the client's consent, in order to maintain his credibility with the jury and to subsequently argue for a life-time sentence, rather than the imposition of the death penalty. Justice Ginsburg noted that "In a capital case, counsel must consider in conjunction both the guilt and penalty phases in determining how best to proceed."

D | *The Right to an Impartial Jury Trial*

In *Apprendi v. New Jesery*, 530 U.S. 466 (2000), the Court struck down a state law permitting judges to hand down longer sentences for "hate crimes" based on the "preponderance of evidence" standard. A bare majority ruled that enhanced sentences may be imposed only by a jury and on the basis of the stricter "beyond a reasonable doubt" standard. That ruling was then extended in *Ring v. Arizona*, 536 U.S. 584 (2002), and in *Blackely v. Washington*, 124 S.Ct. 2531 (2004). In *Blackely*, a bare majority struck down a state sentencing system for permitting judges to make findings that increase a defendant's sentence beyond the ordinary range for violating the Sixth Amendment right to a jury trial. Writing for the Court, Justice Scalia reaffirmed that "any fact that increases the penalty for a crime beyond the prescribed statutory maximum must be submitted to a jury and proved beyond a reasonable doubt." Dissenting Justice O'Connor warned that "Over 20 years of sentencing reform are all but lost," and specifically in jeopardy were the 1987 federal mandatory sentencing guidelines, setting mandatory minimum sentences and adopted as part of the war on crime and to ensure the nationwide application of federal criminal law. Justice O'Connor proved prophetic because in *United States v. Booker*, 125 S.Ct. 738 (2005) a bare majority ruled that the federal guidelines violate the Sixth Amendment because federal judges may impose enhanced sentences based on facts that a jury did not consider.

The Court was badly fragmented in *Booker*, however, and two opinions for the Court were delivered for different bare majorities. On the one hand, Justice Stevens, joined by Justices Scalia, Souter, Thomas, and Ginsburg, ruled that federal judges are no longer bound by the guidelines. On the other hand, Justice Breyer, joined by Chief Justice Rehnquist and Justices O'Connor, Kennedy, and Ginsburg, held that the guidelines should still be consulted and that judges' sentences are subject to reversal if appellate courts find them unreasonable and defendants deserve longer or shorter sentences. The federal guidelines, in the words of Justice Breyer, who helped write them, serve to "avoid excessive sentencing disparities while maintaining flexibility sufficient to individualize sentences where necessary." Justice Ginsburg cast the crucial fifth vote for both opinions but issued no separate opinion. Justices Stevens, Scalia, Thomas, and Breyer, each filed dissenting opinions.

The Court also reaffirmed its ruling in *Batson v. Kentucky*, 476 U.S. 79 (1986) (excerpted in Vol. 2 , Ch. 9) that racial discrimination in the use of preemptory challenges in jury selection is impermissible in *Miller-El v. Dretke*, 125 S.Ct. 2317 (2005). In *Miller-El* the prosecution had "shuffled" 10 of the 11 eligible blacks in the jury pool so as to exclude them from the jury. Writing for the majority, Justice Souter underscored that "when the government's choice of jurors is tainted with racial bias" it jeopardizes "the very integrity of the courts." Dissenting Justice Thomas, joined by Chief Justice Rehnquist and Justice Scalia, argued that practically all of the prosecution's preemptory strikes of blacks could be explained on nonracial grounds. In a related decision, *Johnson v. California*, 125 S.Ct. 2410 (2005), the Court in an eight to one ruling, with Justice Thomas dissenting, held that the California supreme court's standard for showing racial bias, namely, that discrimination was "more likely than not," was too strict under *Batson*. Writing for the Court, Justice Stevens held that defendants need show only a "reasonable inference" of racial bias in the use of preemptory challenges and jury selection.

10

Cruel and Unusual Punishment

B | *Capital Punishment*

Overturning *Stanford v. Kentucky*, 492 U.S. 361 (1989), which upheld the execution of minors convicted of murder under the age of eighteen but older than sixteen, a bare majority of the Court held that the execution of minors violates the Eighth Amendment in *Roper v. Simmons* (excerpted below). The ruling affects approximately seventy death row inmates.

Roper v. Simmons

125 S.Ct. 1183 (2005)

At the age of 17, Christopher Simmons committed murder. About nine months later, after he had turned 18, he was tried and sentenced to death. Before the murder, in chilling, callous terms he talked about his plan, discussing it for the most part with two friends, then aged 15 and 16. Simmons proposed to commit burglary and murder by breaking and entering, tying up a victim, and throwing the victim off a bridge. Simmons assured his friends they could "get away with it" because they were minors. Simmons was later charged with burglary, kidnapping, stealing, and murder. Because Simmons was 17 at the time of the crime, he was outside the criminal jurisdiction of Missouri's juvenile court system. He was tried as an adult, convicted, and sentenced to death. The Missouri Supreme Court affirmed. But, after those proceedings, the U.S.

Supreme Court held that the Eighth and Fourteenth Amendments prohibit the execution of a mentally retarded person. *Atkins v. Virginia*, 536 U.S. 304 (2002). Simmons then filed a new petition for state post-conviction relief, arguing that the reasoning of *Atkins* established that the Constitution prohibits the execution of a juvenile who was under 18 when the crime was committed. The Missouri Supreme Court agreed and held that since *Stanford v. Kentucky*, 492 U.S. 361 (1989), upholding the execution of minors who commit murders, "a national consensus has developed against the execution of juvenile offenders, as demonstrated by the fact that eighteen states now bar such executions for juveniles, that twelve other states bar executions altogether, that no state has lowered its age of execution below 18 since *Stanford*, that five states have legislatively or by case law raised or established the minimum age at 18, and that the imposition of the juvenile death penalty has become truly unusual over the last decade."

The state supreme court's decision was affirmed by a five to four vote. Justice Kennedy delivered the opinion for the Court. Justice Stevens filed a concurring opinion. Justices O'Connor and Scalia filed dissenting opinions; Chief Justice Rehnquist and Justice Thomas joined the latter's dissent.

□ *Justice KENNEDY delivered the opinion of the Court.*

This case requires us to address, for the second time in a decade and a half, whether it is permissible under the Eighth and Fourteenth Amendments to the Constitution of the United States to execute a juvenile offender who was older than 15 but younger than 18 when he committed a capital crime. In *Stanford v. Kentucky*, 492 U.S. 361 (1989), a divided Court rejected the proposition that the Constitution bars capital punishment for juvenile offenders in this age group. We reconsider the question. . . .

The prohibition against "cruel and unusual punishments," like other expansive language in the Constitution, must be interpreted according to its text, by considering history, tradition, and precedent, and with due regard for its purpose and function in the constitutional design. To implement this framework we have established the propriety and affirmed the necessity of referring to "the evolving standards of decency that mark the progress of a maturing society" to determine which punishments are so disproportionate as to be cruel and unusual. *Trop v. Dulles*, 356 U.S. 86 (1958).

In *Thompson v. Oklahoma*, 487 U.S. 815 (1988), a plurality of the Court determined that our standards of decency do not permit the execution of any offender under the age of 16 at the time of the crime. The plurality opinion explained that no death penalty State that had given express consideration to a minimum age for the death penalty had set the age lower than 16. The plurality also observed that "[t]he conclusion that it would offend civilized standards of decency to execute a person who was less than 16 years old at the time of his or her offense is consistent with the views that have been expressed by respected professional organizations, by other nations that share our Anglo-American heritage, and by the leading members of the Western European community."

Bringing its independent judgment to bear on the permissibility of the death penalty for a 15-year-old offender, the *Thompson* plurality stressed that "[t]he reasons why juveniles are not trusted with the privileges and responsibilities of an adult also explain why their irresponsible conduct is not as morally reprehensible as that of an adult." According to the plurality, the lesser culpability of offenders under 16 made the death penalty inappropriate as a form of retribution, while the low likelihood that offenders under 16 engaged in "the kind of cost-benefit analysis that attaches any weight to the possibility of execution" made the death penalty ineffective as a means of deterrence. . . .

The next year, in *Stanford v. Kentucky*, 492 U.S. 361 (1989), the Court, over a dissenting opinion joined by four Justices, referred to contemporary standards of decency in this country and concluded the Eighth and Fourteenth Amendments did not proscribe the execution of juvenile offenders over 15 but under 18. The Court noted that 22 of the 37 death penalty States permitted the death penalty for 16-year-old offenders, and, among these 37 States, 25 permitted it for 17-year-old offenders. These numbers, in the Court's view, indicated there was no national consensus "sufficient to label a particular punishment cruel and unusual." A plurality of the Court also "emphatically reject[ed]" the suggestion that the Court should bring its own judgment to bear on the acceptability of the juvenile death penalty.

The same day the Court decided *Stanford*, it held that the Eighth Amendment did not mandate a categorical exemption from the death penalty for the mentally retarded. *Penry v. Lynaugh*, 492 U.S. 302 (1989). In reaching this conclusion it stressed that only two States had enacted laws banning the imposition of the death penalty on a mentally retarded person convicted of a capital offense.

Three Terms ago the subject was reconsidered in *Atkins* [*v. Virginia*, 536 U.S. 304 (2002)]. We held that standards of decency have evolved since *Penry* and now demonstrate that the execution of the mentally retarded is cruel and unusual punishment. The Court noted objective indicia of society's standards, as expressed in legislative enactments and state practice with respect to executions of the mentally retarded. When *Atkins* was decided only a minority of States permitted the practice, and even in those States it was rare. On the basis of these indicia the Court determined that executing mentally retarded offenders "has become truly unusual, and it is fair to say that a national consensus has developed against it."

The inquiry into our society's evolving standards of decency did not end there. The *Atkins* Court neither repeated nor relied upon the statement in *Stanford* that the Court's independent judgment has no bearing on the acceptability of a particular punishment under the Eighth Amendment. Instead we returned to the rule, established in decisions predating *Stanford*, that "'the Constitution contemplates that in the end our own judgment will be brought to bear on the question of the acceptability of the death penalty under the Eighth Amendment.'" Mental retardation, the Court said, diminishes personal culpability even if the offender can distinguish right from wrong. The impairments of mentally retarded offenders make it less defensible to impose the death penalty as retribution for past crimes and less likely that the death penalty will have a real deterrent effect. Based on these considerations and on the finding of national consensus against executing the mentally retarded, the Court ruled that the death penalty constitutes an excessive sanction for the entire category of mentally retarded offenders, and that the Eighth Amendment "'places a substantive restriction on the State's power to take the life' of a mentally retarded offender."

Just as the *Atkins* Court reconsidered the issue decided in *Penry*, we now reconsider the issue decided in *Stanford*. The beginning point is a review of objective indicia of consensus, as expressed in particular by the enactments of legislatures that have addressed the question. This data gives us essential instruction. We then must determine, in the exercise of our own independent judgment, whether the death penalty is proportionate punishment for juveniles.

The evidence of national consensus against the death penalty for juveniles is similar, and in some respects parallel, to the evidence *Atkins* held sufficient to demonstrate a national consensus against the death penalty for the mentally retarded. When *Atkins* was decided, 30 States prohibited the death penalty for the mentally retarded. This number comprised 12 that had abandoned the death penalty altogether, and 18 that maintained it but excluded the mentally retarded from its reach. By a similar calculation in this case, 30 States prohibit the juvenile death penalty, comprising 12 that have rejected the death penalty altogether and 18 that maintain it but, by express provision or judicial interpretation, exclude juveniles from its reach. *Atkins* emphasized that even in the 20 States without formal prohibition, the practice of executing the mentally retarded was infrequent. Since *Penry*, only five States had executed offenders known to have an IQ under 70. In the present case, too, even in the 20 States without a formal prohibition on executing juveniles, the practice is infrequent. Since *Stanford*, six States have executed prisoners for crimes committed as juveniles. In the past 10 years, only three have done so: Oklahoma, Texas, and Virginia. . . .

Petitioner cannot show national consensus in favor of capital punishment for juveniles but still resists the conclusion that any consensus exists against it. Petitioner supports this position with, in particular, the observation that when the Senate ratified the International Covenant on Civil and Political Rights (ICCPR), Dec. 19, 1966, it did so subject to the President's proposed reservation regarding Article 6(5) of that treaty, which prohibits capital punishment for juveniles. This reservation at best provides only faint support for petitioner's argument. First, the reservation was passed in 1992; since then, five States have abandoned capital punishment for juveniles. Second, Congress considered the issue when enacting the Federal Death Penalty Act in 1994, and determined that the death penalty should not extend to juveniles. The reservation to Article 6(5) of the ICCPR provides minimal evidence that there is not now a national consensus against juvenile executions.

As in *Atkins*, the objective indicia of consensus in this case—the rejection of the juvenile death penalty in the majority of States; the infrequency of its use even where it remains on the books; and the consistency in the trend toward abolition of the practice—provide sufficient evidence that today our society views juveniles, in the words *Atkins* used respecting the mentally retarded, as "categorically less culpable than the average criminal."

A majority of States have rejected the imposition of the death penalty on juvenile offenders under 18, and we now hold this is required by the Eighth Amendment. . . .

Three general differences between juveniles under 18 and adults demonstrate that juvenile offenders cannot with reliability be classified among the worst offenders. First, as any parent knows and as the scientific and sociological studies respondent and his *amici* cite tend to confirm, "[a] lack of maturity and an underdeveloped sense of responsibility are found in youth more often than in adults and are more understandable among the young. These qualities often result in impetuous and ill-considered actions and decisions."

The second area of difference is that juveniles are more vulnerable or susceptible to negative influences and outside pressures, including peer pressure. . . . The third broad difference is that the character of a juvenile is not as well formed as that of an adult. The personality traits of juveniles are more transitory. . . .

Once the diminished culpability of juveniles is recognized, it is evident that the penological justifications for the death penalty apply to them with lesser force than to adults. We have held there are two distinct social purposes served by the death penalty: "'retribution and deterrence of capital crimes by prospective offenders.'" *Atkins*. As for retribution, we remarked in *Atkins* that "[i]f the culpability of the average murderer is insufficient to justify the most extreme sanction available to the State, the lesser culpability of the mentally retarded offender surely does not merit that form of retribution." The same conclusions follow from the lesser culpability of the juvenile offender. . . .

As for deterrence, it is unclear whether the death penalty has a significant or even measurable deterrent effect on juveniles, as counsel for the petitioner acknowledged at oral argument. . . .

Drawing the line at 18 years of age is subject, of course, to the objections always raised against categorical rules. The qualities that distinguish juveniles from adults do not disappear when an individual turns 18. By the same token, some under 18 have already attained a level of maturity some adults will never reach. For the reasons we have discussed, however, a line must be drawn. The plurality opinion in *Thompson* drew the line at 16. In the intervening years the *Thompson* plurality's conclusion that offenders under 16 may not be executed has not been challenged. The logic of *Thompson* extends to those who are under 18. The age of 18 is the point where society draws the line for many purposes between childhood and adulthood. It is, we conclude, the age at which the line for death eligibility ought to rest.

These considerations mean *Stanford v. Kentucky* should be deemed no longer controlling on this issue. . . .

Our determination that the death penalty is disproportionate punishment for offenders under 18 finds confirmation in the stark reality that the United States is the only country in the world that continues to give official sanction to the juvenile death penalty. This reality does not become controlling, for the task of interpreting the Eighth Amendment remains our responsibility. Yet at least from the time of the Court's decision in *Trop*, the Court has referred to the laws of other countries and to international authorities as instructive for its interpretation of the Eighth Amendment's prohibition of "cruel and unusual punishments."

As respondent and a number of *amici* emphasize, Article 37 of the United Nations Convention on the Rights of the Child, which every country in the world has ratified save for the United States and Somalia, contains an express prohibition on capital punishment for crimes committed by juveniles under 18. United Nations Convention on the Rights of the Child, Art. 37, (entered into force Sept. 2, 1990).

Though the international covenants prohibiting the juvenile death penalty are of more recent date, it is instructive to note that the United Kingdom abolished the juvenile death penalty before these covenants came into being. . . .

It is proper that we acknowledge the overwhelming weight of international opinion against the juvenile death penalty, resting in large part on the understanding that the instability and emotional imbalance of young people may often be a factor in the crime. The opinion of the world community, while not controlling our outcome, does provide respected and significant confirmation for our own conclusions.

The Eighth and Fourteenths forbid imposition of the death penalty on offenders who were under the age of 18 when their crimes were committed.

□ *Justice STEVENS, with whom Justice GINSBURG joins, concurring.*

Perhaps even more important than our specific holding today is our reaffirmation of the basic principle that informs the Court's interpretation of the Eighth Amendment. If the meaning of that Amendment had been frozen when it was originally drafted, it would impose no impediment to the execution of 7-year-old children today. See *Stanford v. Kentucky*, 492 U.S. 361 (1989) (describing the common law at the time of the Amendment's adoption). The evolving standards of decency that have driven our construction of this critically important part of the Bill of Rights foreclose any such reading of the Amendment. In the best tradition of the common law, the pace of that evolution is a matter for continuing debate; but that our understanding of the Constitution does change from time to time has been settled since JOHN MARSHALL breathed life into its text. . . .

□ *Justice O'CONNOR, dissenting.*

[T]he Court rests, ultimately, on its independent moral judgment that death is a disproportionately severe punishment for any 17-year-old offender. I do not subscribe to this judgment. Adolescents as a class are undoubtedly less mature, and therefore less culpable for their misconduct, than adults. But the Court has adduced no evidence impeaching the seemingly reasonable conclusion reached by many state legislatures: that at least some 17-year-old murderers are sufficiently mature to deserve the death penalty in an appropriate case. Nor has it been shown that capital sentencing juries are incapable of accurately assessing a youthful defendant's maturity or of giving due weight to the mitigating characteristics associated with youth.

On this record—and especially in light of the fact that so little has changed since our recent decision in *Stanford*—I would not substitute our judgment about the moral propriety of capital punishment for 17-year-old murderers for the judgments of the Nation's legislatures. Rather, I would demand a clearer showing that our society truly has set its face against this practice before reading the Eighth Amendment categorically to forbid it. . . .

□ *Justice SCALIA, with whom THE CHIEF JUSTICE and Justice THOMAS join, dissenting.*

The Court . . . proclaims itself sole arbiter of our Nation's moral standards—and in the course of discharging that awesome responsibility purports to take guidance from the views of foreign courts and legislatures. Because I do not believe that the meaning of our Eighth Amendment, any more than the meaning of other provisions of our Constitution, should be determined by the subjective views of five Members of this Court and like-minded foreigners, I dissent. . . .

Words have no meaning if the views of less than 50% of death penalty States can constitute a national consensus. Our previous cases have required overwhelming opposition to a challenged practice, generally over a long period of time. In *Coker v. Georgia*, 433 U.S. 584 (1977), a plurality concluded the Eighth Amendment prohibited capital punishment for rape of an adult woman where only one jurisdiction authorized such punishment. The plurality also observed that "[a]t no time in the last 50 years ha[d] a majority of States authorized death as a punishment for rape." In *Ford v. Wainwright*, 477 U.S. 399 (1986), we held execution of the insane unconstitutional, tracing the roots of this prohibition to the common law and noting that "no State in the union permits the execution of the insane." In *Enmund v. Florida*, 458 U.S. 782 (1982), we invalidated capital punishment imposed for participation in a robbery in which an accomplice committed murder, because 78% of all death penalty States prohibited this punishment. Even there we expressed some hesitation, because the legislative judgment was "neither 'wholly unanimous among state legislatures,' . . . nor as compelling as the legislative judgments considered in *Coker*." By contrast, agreement among 42% of death penalty States in *Stanford*, which the Court appears to believe was correctly decided at the time was insufficient to show a national consensus. . . .

The Court's reliance on the infrequency of executions, for under-18 Murderers credits an argument that this Court considered and explicitly rejected in *Stanford*. That infrequency is explained, we accurately said, both by "the undisputed fact that a far smaller percentage of capital crimes are committed by persons under 18 than over 18," and by the fact that juries are required at sentencing to consider the offender's youth as a mitigating factor. Thus, "it is not only possible, but overwhelmingly probable, that the very considerations which induce [respondent] and [his] supporters to believe that death should never be imposed on offenders under 18 cause prosecutors and juries to believe that it should rarely be imposed." *Stanford*. . . .

Of course, the real force driving today's decision is . . . the Court's "own judgment" that murderers younger than 18 can never be as morally culpable as older counterparts. The Court claims that this usurpation of the role of moral arbiter is simply a "retur[n] to the rul[e] established in decisions predating *Stanford*." That supposed rule—which is reflected solely in *dicta* and never once in a holding that purports to supplant the consensus of the American people with the Justices' views—was repudiated in *Stanford* for the very good reason that it has no foundation in law or logic. If the Eighth Amendment set forth an ordinary rule of law, it would indeed be the role of this Court to say what the law is. But the Court having pronounced that the Eighth Amendment is an ever-changing reflection of "the evolving standards of decency" of our society, it makes no sense for the Justices then to prescribe those standards rather than discern them from the practices of our people. On the evolving-standards hypothesis, the only legitimate function of this Court is to identify a moral consensus of the American people. By what conceivable warrant can nine lawyers presume to be the authoritative conscience of the Nation? . . .

Though the views of our own citizens are essentially irrelevant to the Court's decision today, the views of other countries and the so-called International community take center stage.

The Court begins by noting that "Article 37 of the United Nations Convention on the Rights of the Child, which every country in the world has ratified save for the United States and Somalia, contains an express prohibition on capital punishment for crimes committed by juveniles under 18."

The Court also discusses the International Covenant on Civil and Political Rights (ICCPR), which the Senate ratified only subject to a reservation that reads: "The United States reserves the right, subject to its Constitutional restraints, to impose capital punishment on any person (other than a pregnant woman) duly convicted under existing or future laws permitting the imposition of capital punishment, including such punishment for crime committed by persons below eighteen years of age." Unless the Court has added to its arsenal the power to join and ratify treaties on behalf of the United States, I cannot see how this evidence favors, rather than refutes, its position. That the Senate and the President—those actors our Constitution empowers to enter into treaties, see Art. II, Sec. 2—have declined to join and ratify treaties prohibiting execution of under-18 offenders can only suggest that our country has either not reached a national consensus on the question, or has reached a consensus contrary to what the Court announces. . . .

More fundamentally, however, the basic premise of the Court's argument—that American law should conform to the laws of the rest of the world—ought to be rejected out of hand. In fact the Court itself does not believe it. In many significant respects the laws of most other countries differ from our law—including not only such explicit provisions of our Constitution as the right to jury trial and grand jury indictment, but even many interpretations of the Constitution prescribed by this Court itself. The Court-pronounced exclusionary rule, for example, is distinctively American. When we adopted that rule in *Mapp v. Ohio*, 367 U.S. 643 (1961), it was "unique to American Jurisprudence." Since then a categorical exclusionary rule has been "universally rejected" by other countries, including those with rules prohibiting illegal searches and police misconduct, despite the fact that none of these countries "appears to have any alternative form of discipline for police that is effective in preventing search violations." England, for example, rarely excludes evidence found during an illegal search or seizure and has only recently begun excluding evidence from illegally obtained confessions. . . . The European Court of Human Rights has held that introduction of illegally seized evidence does not violate the "fair trial" requirement in Article 6, Sec. 1, of the European Convention on Human Rights. . . .

And let us not forget the Court's abortion jurisprudence, which makes us one of only six countries that allow abortion on demand until the point of viability. Though the Government and *amici* in cases following *Roe v. Wade*, 410 U.S. 113 (1973), urged the Court to follow the international community's lead, these arguments fell on deaf ears.

The Court's special reliance on the laws of the United Kingdom is perhaps the most indefensible part of its opinion. It is of course true that we share a common history with the United Kingdom, and that we often consult English sources when asked to discern the meaning of a constitutional text written against the backdrop of 18th-century English law and legal thought. If we applied that approach today, our task would be an easy one. As we explained in *Harmelin v. Michigan*, 501 U.S. 957 (1991), the "Cruell and Unusuall Punishments" provision of the English Declaration of Rights was originally meant to describe those punishments "'out of [the Judges'] Power'"—that is, those punishments that were not authorized by common law or statute, but that were nonetheless administered by the Crown or the Crown's judges. Under that reasoning, the death penalty for under-18 offenders would easily survive this challenge. The Court has, however—I think wrongly—long rejected a purely originalist approach to our Eighth Amendment, and that is certainly not the approach the Court takes today.

Instead, the Court undertakes the majestic task of determining (and thereby prescribing) our Nation's current standards of decency. It is beyond comprehension why we should look, for that purpose, to a country that has developed, in the centuries since the Revolutionary War—and with increasing speed since the United Kingdom's recent submission to the jurisprudence of European courts dominated by continental jurists—a legal, political, and social culture quite different from our own. . . .

The Court should either profess its willingness to reconsider all these matters in light of the views of foreigners, or else it should cease putting forth foreigners' views as part of the reasoned basis of its decisions. To invoke alien law when it agrees with one's own thinking, and ignore it otherwise, is not reasoned decision making, but sophistry. . . .

To add insult to injury, the Court affirms the Missouri Supreme Court without even admonishing that court for its flagrant disregard of our precedent in *Stanford*. Until today, we have always held that "it is this Court's prerogative alone to overrule one of its precedents." That has been true even where " 'changes in judicial doctrine' ha[ve] significantly undermined" our prior holding, and even where our prior holding "appears to rest on reasons rejected in some other line of decisions." Today, however, the Court silently approves a state-court decision that blatantly rejected controlling precedent. . . .

Allowing lower courts to reinterpret the Eighth Amendment whenever they decide enough time has passed for a new snapshot leaves this Court's decisions without any force—especially since the "evolution" of our Eighth Amendment is no longer determined by objective criteria. To allow lower courts to behave as we do, "updating" the Eighth Amendment as needed, destroys stability and makes our case law an unreliable basis for the designing of laws by citizens and their representatives, and for action by public officials. The result will be to crown arbitrariness with chaos.

II

The Right of Privacy

A | *Privacy and Reproductive Freedom*

In its 2005-2006 term, the Court will revisit the constitutionality of parental consent laws for minors who seek an abortion in *Ayotte v. Planned Parenthood of Northern New England* (No. 04-1144). At issue is the constitutionality of New Hampshire's law requiring abortion providers to give a minor's parents 48 hours notice before the procedure, unless a judge grants an exception or girl's life is at risk. Some 33 states have a parental notice or consent law and eight states have laws similar to New Hampshire's. Unlike most other parental consent laws, it makes no exception for cases in which the health of a pregnant girl is at risk. In addition, another question raised is what standard courts should use in reviewing challenges to abortion laws that have not yet taken effect. In striking down New Hampshire's law, a federal appellate court relied on *Planned Parenthood of Southeastern Pennsylvania v. Casey*, 505 U.S. 833 (1992) (excerpted in Vol. 2, Chapter 11), which struck down a provision requiring women to notify their husbands before obtaining an abortion. Although the majority found that in most cases married women consult with their husbands, the law posed an "undue burden" on the approximately one percent of women who do not want to notify their husbands. The Court of Appeals for the First Circuit applied that analysis in striking down New Hampshire's provision. It reasoned that even if most pregnant teenagers do not have health problems requiring the termination of their pregnancies, the law's requirements pose "an undue burden" on those who suffer certain medical conditions, such as a premature membrane rupture. On that basis, the appellate court held the law unconstitutional and enjoined its enforcement. In appealing that decision, state attorney general Kelly A. Ayotte argues that courts should issue injunctions against the enforcement of laws that have not yet taken effect only when "no set of circumstances exists under which the act would be valid," a less rigorous standard than employed by the appellate court and suggested in *Casey*.

12

The Equal Protection of the Laws

A | *Racial Discrimination and State Action*

In *Johnson v. California*, 125 S.Ct. 2410 (2005), the Court held that the "strict scrutiny" test applies in cases of racially segregated prison cells, but declined to decide whether California's prison policy of segregating inmates failed to satisfy that test. Wring for the Court, Justice O'Connor observed: "By perpetuating the notion that race matters, racial segregation of inmates may exacerbate the very patterns of violence that it is said to counteract. In the prison context, when the government's power is at its apex, we think that searching judicial review of racial classifications is necessary to guard against invidious discrimination." In a separate opinion, joined by Justices Souter and Breyer, Justice Ginsburg agreed but indicated that the use of racial classifications may be permissible in order to wipe out "entrenched discrimination and its after-effects." Justice Stevens dissented and contended that the majority should have gone farther and struck down California's policy. In a separate dissent joined by Justice Scalia, Justice Thomas countered that the majority should have deferred to California prison officials in managing their prison populations, observing that "The Constitution has always demanded less within the prison walls."

D | *Nonracial Classifications and the Equal Protection of the Law*

(4) *Alienage and Age*

■ The Development of Law

Rulings on the Classification of Aliens

CASE	VOTE	RULING
Jama v. Immigration and Customs Enforcement, 125 S.Ct. 694 (2005)	5:4	Writing for the Court, Justice Scalia held that a refugee living in the United States may be deported after a criminal conviction to the home country, even without the consent of that country's government. Justices Souter, Stevens, Ginsburg, and Breyer dissented.
Clark v. Martinez, 125 S.Ct. 716 (2005)	7:2	Writing for the Court, and drawing on the ruling in *Zadvydas v. Davis*, U.S. 678 (2001), holding that aliens may be detained for six months as "reasonably necessary" to effectuate their removal, Justice Scalia held that inadmissible aliens may be held six months or longer, as "reasonably necessary," even if they may not be returned to their home country. Chief Justice Rehnquist and Justice Thomas dissented.

Index of Cases

Cases printed in boldface are excerpted on the page(s) printed in boldface.

Other Books by David M. O'Brien

Storm Center:
The Supreme Court in American Politics
7th ed.

Constitutional Law and Politics:
Vol. 1. *Struggles for Power and Governmental Accountability*
Vol. 2. *Civil Rights and Civil Liberties*
6th ed.

Animal Sacrifice and Religious Freedom:
Church of Lukumi Babalu Aye v. City of Hialeah

Judicial Roulette

What Process Is Due?
Courts and Science-Policy Disputes

The Public's Right to Know:
The Supreme Court and the First Amendment

Privacy, Law, and Public Policy

Judges on Judging: Views from the Bench
2nd ed. (editor)

To Dream of Dreams:
Religious Freedom and Constitutional Politics in Postwar Japan
(with Yasuo Ohkoshi)

Abortion and American Politics
(with Barbara H. Craig)

Judicial Independence in the Age of Democracy:
Critical Perspectives from Around the World
(edited with Peter Russell)

The Politics of Technology Assessment:
Institutions, Processes and Policy Disputes
(edited with Donald Marchand)

Views from the Bench:
The Judiciary and Constitutional Politics
(edited with Mark Cannon)

The Politics of American Government
3d ed.
(with Stephen J. Wayne, G. Calvin Mackenzie, and Richard Cole)

Government by the People
21st ed.
(with David B. Magleby, Paul Light, James MacGregor Burns,
J. W. Peltason, and Thomas E. Cronin)